THE TECHNIQUE
OF
SEA FISHING

THE TECHNIQUE
OF
SEA FISHING

Written and Illustrated by
W. E. DAVIES

Contributor to *Trout and Salmon*, *Irish Stream
and Field*, *Chasse et Pêche* etc.

PAPERFRONTS
ELLIOT RIGHT WAY BOOKS
KINGSWOOD, SURREY, U.K.

CONTENTS

CONTENTS

ILLUSTRATIONS

CHAPTER I

INTRODUCTORY

Of all the varied types of angling none holds greater fascination than sea fishing. If this were not true, the sport which has on more than one occasion been claimed the most health-giving of all, would not be followed by so many. Nor would there be so insistent a demand for knowledge of the fundamentals of this kind of fishing. It breathes an air of repose and satisfaction, a spirit which when it refers to outward circumstances is called contentment, and when one refers to oneself is called complacency. Sea anglers, in fact, do not think ill of themselves, and of their sport they think exceedingly well.

It is a branch of angling which has attracted the largest number of votaries. The small boy, out at elbows, catches his small whiting or pollack by the aid of a handline from the pier or rocks with the same zest as the owner of a powered boat his 500-lb. tunny. The real pleasure is in the excitement of the catch, not in the size or delicacy of the prey, the latter points merely adding the relish which is at times required to prevent satiety.

From the time when the whale swallowed Jonah, the fish has played no inconsiderable part in human affairs, without taking into consideration its value from a culinary point of view. Be that as it may it is often assumed by the uninitiated that sea fishing is more of a wholesale butchering of fish than a sporting pastime.

In sea fishing, whether it be from rocks, beach, pier or boat the man who catches more fish than his fellows is usually one who has the capacity for taking pains – not only in the big matters but more so in the minor things. Above all else he makes a careful study of fish, their habits and reactions to the varying conditions of their restless habitat.

Such a man inevitably becomes a specialist for the simple reason that he leaves nothing to chance. For instance, he notes the topography of the shoreline and the flow of currents, phases of the moon, the times of the tides and last but not least, he invests in a survey chart of the coastal area he intends to fish.

Such a chart will assist in finding fishing spots by indication of depth at low and high tide and the nature and formation of the sea-bed. Such knowledge is half the battle when going sea fishing and does away with that tiresome method of trial and error.

For centuries men have been catching fish with rod and line around our coasts but it was not until 1893 that sea angling was put on an organised basis. In that year the British Sea Anglers Society was formed following a meeting in London of a number of enthusiastic fishermen. Since that time a big industry has been built around the sport until today there is hardly a spot around our coasts where an angler is not catered for with boats, tackle, baits, etc.

As in all kinds of fishing the sea angler will experience good days and bad ones, despite the fact that the sea, we are assured by the experts, swarms with fish.

As you get to know the sea better you will find that Nature is less variable in her external appearances on land than on the sea, which on a grey day does not seem to be the same element as that which effervesces and sparkles when the sun is shining. The transition from light to shadow affects not merely the colour, but the form and substance, and the billows of emerald become with change of cloud inert ridges of lead.

On other occasions the sea is broken and ragged, its blackish-green having the sinister effect of some concealed tragedy as sunrise puts a red wedge under the inky clouds which droop along the horizon; now blue and flashing with a jocund brilliancy, the ships scooping their way through it with a conscious sportiveness; and then pallid and vague, a phantom sea with ghostly ships. However, unlike the fresh-water angler who is handicapped or otherwise by weather conditions, the sea angler can follow his sport throughout the many and varied moods of the sea.

For years now there has been a great deal of discussion between freshwater anglers and those who fish the salty waters of the sea as to which branch is superior. The question is extremely difficult for anyone to determine, as the enjoyment derived from either branch of angling depends to a large extent upon the individual and the type of tackle he may use in catching a particular species of fish. For several years I was of the opinion that catching a fresh run salmon was superior to anything else in the rod and tackle game, but that was before I tried conclusions with sea bass. Now I am at the cross-roads and just cannot say which is best. It is just one of those things best left to the individual to find out for himself.

In recent years it has pleased me considerably to note the trend towards lightweight tackle. The true sportsman will always try his best to use tackle that will give him the greatest pleasure in fighting a game fish and at the same time give the fish a fair chance. No man, expert or novice, will ever derive the utmost fun from fishing until he has reached the point where he considers the battle far superior to the catch.

For me, and I dare say there are thousands like me, the fascination of sea fishing lies in the uncertainty of the size of your catch and the type of fish. I feel confident that non-anglers who enjoy a holiday at the seaside would derive more benefit if they hired a rod and tackle and went fishing. A day or two sea fishing will be found to act as a sedative to jaded nerves and tired brains. Even after years of sea fishing the writer still thrills at the strike of a mackerel at an artificial fly. Among fish, the mackerel is one of Nature's best examples of streamlining. Built for touring, it ranges all around our coasts. Like so many summer tourists, the reason for its wanderings are not fully understood, but very evidently these long-distance swims keep it in good fighting trim, for the mackerel can, and will, give the fisherman equipped with light tackle one of those fishing thrills to be remembered.

About the food value of this fish little need be said. It is one of the staples of the fishing industry, and incidentally will hold its own at any gastronomic tournament. Some time, try baking a mackerel that is just out of the water. Put it in a pan with some fat, sprinkle with pepper and salt, and bake for about twenty-five minutes in a hot oven. There's another thrill to be remembered – and what a tonic for the worst case of depression-nerves!

Of course with the exception of the tunny we have no giant game fish like those which inhabit the waters around Florida, South Africa and Australia but why worry when we have such tackle testers as tope, conger, skate, halibut, ling, coalfish, pollack, blue shark, turbot, and last but not least, bass.

THE TOLL OF INDUSTRY

As the writer sees it, more and more freshwater anglers will be taking up sea fishing in the future than ever before and the reason for it is not far to seek. Many a river and stream, which not so many years ago, teemed with fish, is now dead. They have either been fished to a standstill or killed by pollution.

Coincidental with the dearth of fishable waters, there has been a tremendous increase in the number of anglers. Unscientific restocking and pollution have resulted in a shortage of freshwater fishing facilities without parallel in our angling history.

Industrial growth has caused the unnecessary death of millions of fish and the defilement of thousands of miles of water. Nature, unaided, is powerless to stand the strain. We have a few privately owned fish hatcheries in various parts of the country, but to the present there is no State fish farm. Serious attention to the twin problems of restocking and pollution is long overdue so is it any wonder that freshwater anglers are turning to the sea for their sport?

For easy classification our sea fish are divided into three groups: (1) top feeders like the mackerel, bass and mullet; (2) middle water feeders such as pollack, coalfish and bream, and (3) the bottom fish like the cod, haddock, hake, ling, whiting, plaice, dab, sole, flounder, skate, tope, conger, gurnards and pouting.

Of the sporting species I think the bass takes pride of place with the mackerel, pollack, coalfish, tope and mullet in close support.

In the heavyweight class the skate is well in front; fish of over 300-lb. down to 200-lb. having been recorded as being caught on rod and line since 1910, but for these giants special tackle is needed. Next we have the halibut, the record weight of which stands at the moment at 197-lb., with others recorded of over 100-lb. Conger is third with a grand fish of 102-lb.

In the light-heavyweight section we have tope, best of which range from over 70-lb. to 50-lb., monkfish 66-lb., ling 50-lb., cod 53-lb. For the middleweight there are coalfish, pollack, bull huss, and turbot all of which are recorded over the 20-lb. mark. For the welterweight class the angler can expect gurnard, john dory, bass, haddock, mullet and plaice. Lightweights are mackerel, pouting, sole, whiting, wrasse, flounder, bream (red and black) and dab.

On looking through the records one finds that Ireland holds those relating to several fish, pouting, blue shark and skate. England is the holder in respect of conger, coalfish, hake, mullet, plaice, ling, mackerel, john dory, pollack, sole, tope, turbot, wrasse, gurnard, flounder and whiting. Scotland is represented with the halibut.

ARE YOU LUCKY?

Providing one is in the right spot and using the proper bait hooking a record fish is purely luck, it is the playing and landing that takes the skill and the best plan of campaign for a beginner to embark upon is to join a sea angling society and make friends with those members who have a few years of sea fishing experience behind them.

It is a simple matter to stand on a rock or pier and cast into the sea a paternoster or ledger, but the bait on the hooks may not be suitable for the species of fish that inhabit that area, then again the weights may not be suitable, therefore it is easy to understand the importance of obtaining local knowledge.

Casting a baited sea tackle requires quite a bit of skill and can only be achieved after hours of practice.

Boat fishing is in a class by itself for different tactics and in some cases tackle have to be employed. A good boatman is essential and by that I do not imply one that can handle a boat expertly, but rather one that not only is an expert with a boat, but also knows where to anchor for the best sport. Believe me there are quite a number of boatmen around our coasts who can manage a boat in all kinds of weather, but have little or no knowledge of the habits of sea fish. So in selecting a boatman be sure he is also a fisherman.

On checking my diaries I find that my best dabs were taken at Cromer and Gorleston (Norfolk); Southend, Leigh-on-Sea and Bradwell-on-Sea (Essex); Hastings, Bexhill, New-haven, and Brighton (Sussex); Brixham, Dartmouth, Exmouth and Torquay (Devon). In each case the chart for the district concerned indicates a sea-bed largely composed of sand and shingle which these fish like.

The rocky characteristic of the sea bed at Dover and Folkestone (Kent); Bognor and Eastbourne (Sussex); Bridport, Poole and Weymouth (Dorset); Clovelly and Ilfracombe (Devon); and Port Issac (Cornwall) was excellent for pollack.

On the other hand the shallow creeks which abound at Broadstairs, Ramsgate and Herne Bay (Kent); Budleigh Salterton and Plymough (Devon); Falmouth and Penzance (Cornwall) suited grey mullet.

However, after years of wandering and experimenting with one place and another my preference is for that part of the Cornish coast – from the Lizard Light to the Longships Light, a mile off Land's End. It is approximately twenty-five miles between these two points, but the coast-line is more than fifty miles in length and embraces some of the grandest fishing of which this country can boast.

Between the two peninsulars of the Lizard and Land's End has been created the Mount's Bay which has often been described as the "English Mecca" of sea anglers.

Some idea as to what it is capable of producing can be gauged from the fact that skate of 160-lb. and over have been taken. Cod 25-lb., ling 31-lb., pollack 17-lb., and pouting 3-lb. Regarding conger, fish of 30-lb. and over are fairly common. The whole of the Bay is good for mackerel and I have had good sport when using artificial fly for them during midsummer.

In Wales, the best spots for general fishing are around Pwllheli, Anglesey, Barmouth, Swansea and Tenby.

In Scotland practically the whole of the west coast is good with Ross and Sutherland excellent, indeed the biggest plaice, whiting, pollack, and cod that have come my way were caught while boat fishing off the Ross coast.

The Isle of Man provides good fishing and my best sport

has been obtained just off Douglas, Peel, Ramsay and Port Erin, but there are many others well worth prospecting. The thing I like about boat fishing off this island is that the boat charges are fixed by the Harbour Commissioners and are uniform and cheap.

For the man who is anxious for big fish as well as variety he cannot do better than visit Ballycotton (Ireland). The only snag is that accommodation is very limited and application has to be made months in advance. There is hardly a season passes but several skate of over 100-lb. each are landed, with conger ranging from 15-lb. to 30-lb., ling up to 20-lb. and pollack over 12-lb. In addition, one can hire tackle and harness to go after the sharks. Bream, gurnard and haddock, etc., grow to a large size.

Natives of this fishing village have no superiors as sailors and fishermen, and visitors need have no fear of embarking in a local fishing boat.

Other good centres in the "Green Isle" include Ardmore, Youghal, Ballinskelligs, Valentia, Achill, Westport and Kinsale, with many others that the writer has not as yet visited.

CHAPTER II

RODS, REELS AND LINES

Many a fishing holiday has been ruined because of a hastily-made decision to purchase a rod, reel and line which has turned out to be quite unsuitable for the type of fishing intended. It is always best to think well before making a final decision.

For the man who would prefer fishing from the beach or pier it is essential that he learn to cast long distances. Therefore the rod should have plenty of backbone and be a little longer than that which would be needed for fishing from a boat. If money is no object there is nothing to beat a built cane rod for each of the two types of fishing. I have a couple of built cane rods and also two made of greenheart and strangely enough the rods I like to handle best are the greenhearts. They are both over twenty years old and when new cost but £1.50 each. Today greenheart is difficult to obtain, but science has invented another material, which lends itself admirably to the making of rods; it is fibre glass. A sea fishing rod made of this material is not affected by salt water to the same extent as those made of built cane, steel or greenheart.

For beach casting solid or hollow built fibre glass rods make excellent tools. There is, however, one drawback to solid fibre glass rods, they are heavy and can be very tiring if there is much casting to be done. To the novice I would suggest hollow glass for beach casting and solid glass for boat fishing when after tope, shark or conger.

BUY WISELY

There are many inferior kinds of fibre glass to get so it

pays to get a rod from a reputable dealer. Then again some makers put on cheap fittings and within a few weeks the angler who has purchased such a rod finds that the supposed stainless steel rings are just plated and beginning to show signs of rust. Don't be put off by salesmanship talk, for the chances are that the individual "painting" such glowing pictures knows very little about fishing. A good rod costs money, but it is an investment and with a little care will give years of lasting enjoyment.

YOU NEVER KNOW

In boat fishing you never know when you may not be at one end of a line with a hundredweight skate at the other, even so, a little taper in the rod will help considerably in bringing your catch to gaff. The "give" of a rod (arc) is based on an engineering principle and while the pressure it exerts on the fish is only a few pounds it is sufficient to beat the greatest gamesters of the sea. A few years ago the Governor of South Australia, Sir Willoughby Norrie, defeated a white pointer shark which weighed 2,224 pounds, one of the heaviest fish ever killed by rod. This record has since been beaten.

The line Sir Willoughby Norrie was using was 162-lb. breaking strain yet he whipped that giant fish in just over two hours. This gives some idea of the pressure that can be exerted by a properly built rod coupled with proper braking of the reel.

Of course we have nothing in the fish species swimming around our coasts which approach that weight – or have we?

For big fish the rings should be buttressed with non-corrosive steel fittings as there is less danger of them cracking when dropped or accidentally hit by the gaff.

On my rods the end ring is what is known as a tulip and is one of the best kinds for preventing fouling of the line when wet.

The reel seats are of phosphor bronze which is impervious

to the corroding action of sea water. Brass is all right, but aluminium is useless. Following an accident in which my reel slipped out of the seat into the sea when boat fishing I had screw type seats fitted and have never regretted it. All sea rods should be fitted with them, and there would be fewer lost tempers.

REELS

For beach, rock or pier fishing a reel capable of holding 150 yards of line is needed and here again there should be no aluminium in its make-up. An ideal reel (if you can afford it) is one made of non-corrosive Duralumin with the spindle of polished cast steel and the bearing of phosphor bronze. Such a reel will last a life-time with careful use. However, it is a costly item and today there are several makes of reels on the market that can be relied upon to answer very well.

THE BEST IS ALWAYS CHEAPEST

For years the four inch Nottingham (wood) reel was part of my equipment when fishing from pier or beach and an eight inch Scarborough reel (wood) for boat and deep water work. The flange and fittings on each were of brass and they met every demand made upon them. In recent years we have passed through the plastic age and tackle manufacturers seized upon the idea of bakelite and plastic treated fibroid reels, with no doubt the idea of greater mass production and the cutting down in weight of the reel. A bakelite reel has one great drawback, it breaks easily. A slight knock will chip it and if it is dropped on a rock it will crack in all probability beyond repair. The fibroid reel in the smaller sizes is very good, but in the larger reels tends to be heavy and cumbersome, but they are definitely superior to the old type wooden reels.

My advice is purchase one of the large modern fixed spool reels or a multiplier like the Ambassadeur 6000 for beach

ROD ACCESSORIES

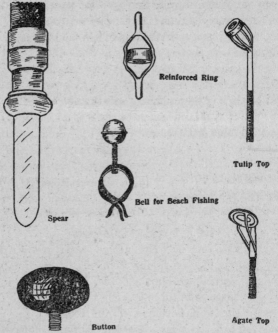

Reinforced Ring

Tulip Top

Bell for Beach Fishing

Spear

Button

Agate Top

fishing and a large multiplier of the Penn type for heavy-weight boat work. In regard to the Ambassadeur reel it is one of the best reels of its kind I have ever owned, what is more I use it not only for beach fishing, but also for spinning for mackerel, pollack and salmon and sea trout. It is a general purpose reel any angler can be proud of.

Always remember to give your reels a good oiling before starting off for a day's fishing and on returning dismantle them and with an oily rag give them a good cleaning. You will be surprised at the amount of dirt and sand that has found its way underneath the flange.

On occasions a fixed spool reel or a multiplier is handy to spin for mackerel, pollack, bass and coalfish and if the reel has any aluminium in its fittings give the parts a good coat of oil before using to protect them from sea water and at the conclusion of your day's fishing give it a thorough cleaning, finishing off with another coat of oil. The rod for this work can be the same as that used for sea trout spinning and if the mackerel are feeding near the surface a trout rod is ideal as the mackerel is given a chance to show what a sporting fish it is. But remember when using freshwater tackle in salt water to cover all aluminium with a coating of oil.

LINES

Sea anglers evince just as much taste in selecting a line as their most fastidious brothers of river and lake. The novice should bear in mind when purchasing his sea lines that the lighter they are the smaller the weight needed to keep bottom. Lines are made of flax, braided and plaited nylon and nylon monofilm. Twisted or "cable-laid" lines are the strongest, but tend to kink more easily than the more expensive plaited lines. Since 1939 we have had nylon which is both cheap and serviceable. Until the advent of nylon my reels carried cutty-hunk (flax) lines of 15-lb. breaking strain for general beach, pier and rock fishing with a 24-lb. line for light boat work. Today my lines are of the same breaking strain, but are braided nylon while the line used for spinning is a 4-lb. nylon monofilm for mackerel and 8-lb. monofilm for pollack, coalfish and bass.

Monofilm deserves its many advocates in strengths up to 8-lbs. but in the heavier strengths it is inclined to be much too springy and difficult to handle, especially on a fixed spool reel.

Nylon has one great advantage over other line making materials in that it does not rot no matter how long in use. However, for really big fish, such as skate, conger, etc., I stick to cuttyhunk because there is less elasticity in it than nylon and as a result more pounds pressure can be applied direct to the hook before the line stretches.

However, no matter what material the line is made of, at the end of a day's fishing it should be transferred to a line-dryer and given a wash in fresh water to get rid of the salt crystals. Although nylon is impervious to salt water, salt crystals can do quite a bit of damage, particularly in the case of braided nylon. The crystals work their way in among the nylon threads and act as an abrasive when the line is under pressure from a fighting fish. As the angler "pumps" his fish the line retrieved is reeled in and it is during the pressure exerted by the rod against the line that the crystals get in their fell work, before they are melted by the action of the salt water.

For float fishing nylon monofilm is ideal in the lower strengths and for big fish braided nylon will be found to answer much better than a flax line. A flax line water-logs much quicker than either of the others no matter how much it is dressed. In float fishing there is nothing so annoying as a line that sinks. In the first place the angler's strike is slowed up by the loop of submerged line and secondly an undue strain is put on the rod top.

For deep-sea fishing for sharks there are now fine gauge metal lines of considerable strength.

CHAPTER III

GENERAL TACKLE AND BAITS

To complete the equipment, hooks, leads (weights), ledgers, traces, paternosters and one or two other items are required. We will take hooks first.

HOOKS

These can be purchased loose to be made up into paternosters and ledgers when needed or one can purchase the tackle already armed with hooks. When the author first started he used to purchase his tackles, but after a while found it quite an easy matter to construct both paternosters and ledgers.

For flat fish (plaice, flounders, sole, etc.), long shanked hooks are best as they facilitate the job of getting the hook out of a fish; for most other species short shanks are better. Taken in retrospect the hook is a small and rather humble bit of fishing gear and yet it is among the most important articles in the tackle bag. You can have the most expensive rod and reel and the finest line but your fishing creel will remain untenanted if your hook fails you.

How many fish hooks there are differing in size, shape and finish is not recorded, but there are hundreds, probably several thousands. For general bottom fishing there are three types that should be among your equipment, they are *Kirby*, *Limerick* and *Carlisle*. They should be eyed and vary in size (Redditch Scale) from o to 4, but be sure and purchase an equal number of short and long shanks.

You will note that Kirby is placed first. That is done

deliberately because the pull of this type of hook is most direct, gives the best penetration and is also stronger. For paternostering it is the ideal hook. For ledgering Limerick and Carlisle are best because of the wider gape between the point of the hook and the shank.

When you buy hooks don't assume that they are sharp. From the time they leave the maker until they are purchased they have been knocked about quite a lot and the point on any hook is a most delicate thing and is easily dulled. Therefore give the point of each hook a little hand honing. Sharp hooks pay dividends in holding the fish for if the hook is good and sharp it is hardly necessary to strike a fish hard. It will set the hook itself due to the drag of the line.

Besides being kept sharp, hooks should always be kept rust free. It is well therefore to rub your hooks with an oily rag after using them.

LEADS

There are numerous types of leads but for the best kinds see illustration titled "Lead Sea Weights". The "N.B. Holdfast", Sectional Deal and Round Flat are best for use with paternoster and ledger with the Spiral for float fishing and the last two for beach casting.

A friend of mine, the late Mr. A. W. C. Copping who for twenty years was Commodore of the Dreadnought (London) Sea Angler's Society, some years ago told me an easy method of making weights of various sizes. It is quite simple for all that is required are a few mussel shells of different size and some damp sand to hold them. The shells act as moulds. Place a shell in the sand, pour a little molten lead in, then place a loop of stainless steel wire in so that the loop just hangs over a pointed end then continue filling the shell with liquid lead. In five minutes it will be cool enough to leave the mould.

If unable to obtain shells good moulds can be made from hollowing out a half of a potato to the shape required. The potato mould is then placed in the sand, wire loop put in position and the lead is poured in.

LEAD SEA WEIGHTS

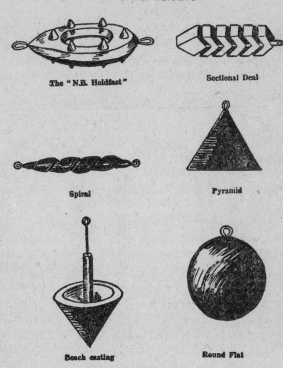

The " N.B. Holdfast "

Sectional Deal

Spiral

Pyramid

Beach casting

Round Flat

LEDGERS

Once you have a pattern it is a simple matter to make your own ledgers, therefore I do not propose to describe their make-up, only their uses. The ledger is an ideal tackle for conger, flat fish and deep swimming bass. The paternoster is the most widely used tackle of any in salt water and is best made with stainless steel wire although quite a few of my friends use brass, and nylon monofilmament.

PATERNOSTERS

With paternosters one can have them equipped with one, two or even three hooks. General practice is for a two hooked one for beach fishing and from pier or rocks because it is much more easy to cast with, and three hooks for boat work.

PREVENTING GAFF ACCIDENTS

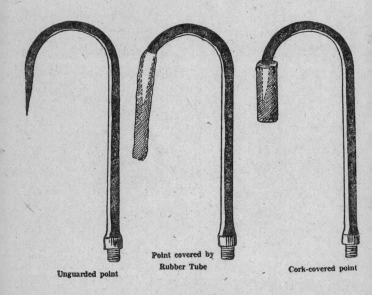

Unguarded point   Point covered by Rubber Tube   Cork-covered point

TRACES

For large fish like conger, skate, etc., a wire trace is necessary for the terminal tackle. A trace connects the tackle to the line with swivels and these should be a dull colour. A few extra swivels in the tackle box will always come in handy.

THREE BOOM WIRE PATERNOSTER

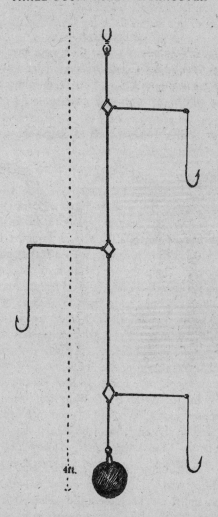

4ft.

GAFF

For conger, skate, cod and other big fish a gaff is a necessity at all times. Purchase a gaff that has a standard thread on the base so that it will fit in the handle of the net. With a gaff it is a wise precaution to keep the point covered. A piece of rubber tubing that fits tightly to the gaff is all right, but the best safeguard against accidents is to take the gaff to an engineer and have him put a thread on the point that will take a small nut. With such a safety device there is no danger of anyone getting a nasty wound. It is an easy matter to unscrew the nut (remembering of course the pocket you put it in) when the gaff is not in use.

FLOATS

These are mostly used when pier and rock fishing for bass and mullet and the one most in evidence today is the sliding float which can be anything from four to seven inches. A float with which I have had quite a good bit of sport among bass when pier fishing is the one that is made of celluloid with a hole running through the middle of its length. Another type of sliding float has brass rings fixed to the side of the float body. For really deep water work they are good, but for shallow inshore fishing a fixed float is superior and the one which answers all requirements is that where the float body is cut to allow admission of the line while the wooden shaft fits tight thus keeping the line in position. With such a float it is an easy matter to take it off or put it on the tackle, and after all simplicity is the keynote of all good angling tackle.

In float fishing the line should be kept well greased. The size of the float to be used will depend to a large degree on the amount of weight used. The less weight the smaller the float required.

LANDING NET

For the ordinary type of sea fishing a landing net is a most

 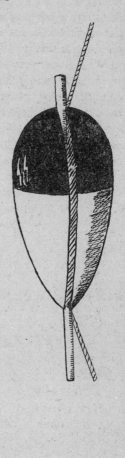

essential part of one's tackle and it should have a fairly long handle, 5 ft. is not too long when pier or rock fishing. The handle should be fairly stout so that it can be used as the gaff handle when required.

LINE-DRYER

This little gadget can be bought for very little and will last a lifetime. It is needed for all types of lines after the day's fishing is over. To use such lines and not have a line-dryer to run them on at the end of the day brings to mind that old adage of "a penny wise and pound foolish".

FISHING BAG

Years ago the sea angler used to saunter forth equipped with a large wicker basket, but times have changed and in these days the bag most in use is made of canvas. Old Army heavy duty canvas packs are the very thing as they have two pockets in which reels and other tackle can be put. They can be purchased at any Army surplus stores. In order to keep the inside of the bag free from fishy smells (providing you catch some fish) it is an easy matter to make a washable lining. All you need is a yard of plastic material sold in most stores for use as bathroom curtains. At the end of the day's fishing just take out the lining and wash it and in a few minutes it will be dry and can be replaced.

BAITS (NATURAL)

When a freshwater angler heads for the coast on a fishing holiday he usually fills his tackle bag with all manner of things calculated to catch fish. On arrival at the coast town he visits a local tackle shop. Tackle dealers usually sell the baits for which there is a demand without ascertaining their actual effectiveness. They, too, assume that baits for which there is a demand are the ones that are most effective, else the anglers would not continue to purchase them.

NATURAL BAITS

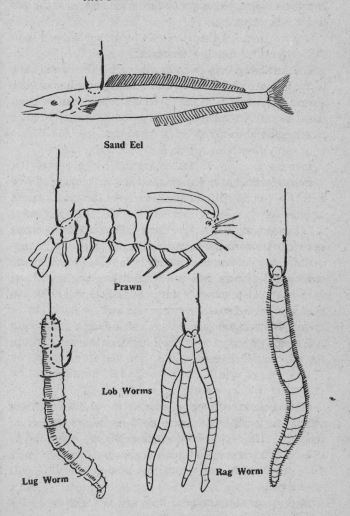

Sand Eel

Prawn

Lob Worms

Lug Worm

Rag Worm

The list of good baits mainly used by anglers fishing from the shore, piers and jetties and fishing from an anchored boat is not too long to remember. They include fish, shellfish and crustaceans. Also there are various kinds of sand worms. It is well to remember that at certain periods of the year most fish prefer shell fish and crustaceans to fish flesh and vice versa. This is one thing many anglers seem either not to know or to disregard. It is also well to remember that most baits acceptable to fish in the area you are fishing can be easily found if you have the proper equipment. Likewise, it should be remembered that fresh bait is better than stale bait, and an hour spent in catching it is an hour well spent.

In most cases you'll catch more and bigger fish on live bait than on dead bait. This means that you should know how to hook live bait so that it remains lively for the greater length of time.

Let us look at this bait question a little more closely listing the various ones in alphabetical order.

Crabs are good for quite a number of species including bass, codling and whiting. It is best when it has cast its shell and at that period is known as a soft crab. They should be hooked near the pointed end on either side and not through the middle. After the tide has receded a walk along a rocky beach will always provide a few. Small hermit crabs are good bait for cod, whiting, haddock and flat fish, but are more difficult to find as they live in discarded whelk shells. But a search at low tide might reveal a few.

Earthworms are no use whatsoever in the sea as the salt water kills them, but are very good for estuary fishing for flounders. The best worm for this is the lob which can be collected from lawns and fields at night after a shower of rain. They should be hooked through the head to allow for plenty of wriggling.

Limpets are not very good baits and are only used when

nothing else is available. Any rock that is washed by the sea will have dozens on. They can easily be removed with the blade of a knife. The hook should be placed through the soft part with only the point entering the hard portion which is the limpet's muscle.

Lugworms are without a doubt one of the best all round baits known and as they are easy to obtain, can be used whole or in pieces and will take all manner of fish. In length they range from three inches to seven inches. To collect a supply go out with a spade immediately the tide has gone out. Dotted about over the face of the damp sand will be dozens of worm casts. Dig a little to one side of the cast and at a depth of about a foot or eighteen inches you will locate the worm. They can be kept fresh several days if they are placed in a bucket of water.

Mudworms more commonly called ragworms are also a good general bait, but are not so easy to come by as the former as the places they inhabit are usually mudflats laved by the sea. Grey mullet and plaice are particularly fond of this worm.

Mackerel, the flesh of this fish is good bait for quite a number of fish including cod, conger, skate, whiting and tur-bot while a whole mackerel is excellent for conger, tope and sharks. A piece of skin from near the tail (see illustration) is good for bass during the summer. This type of bait is called a lask and should be made from a fresh mackerel. It is best when used from a moving boat.

Mussel, this in my humble opinion is the best bait of all for the smaller species of sea fish. It is more than twenty years since I learned the secret of the mussel, and after I found out I wondered at my stupidity at not discovering it sooner. Maybe it wasn't so stupid after all, because I've passed the secret on to hundreds of fishers since then who have been berating their poor luck. After removing the mussel from its shell you turn it inside out and then put it on the hook. As it bleeds into the surrounding water it attracts the fish. In the case of mullet, pollack, bass and coalfish it makes them voracious. It is a good idea to collect

MAKING A LASK

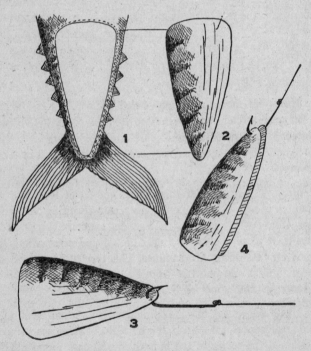

a supply of mussels and place them in a bucket in which there is a plentiful supply of fresh damp seaweed. In such a container they will keep alive for days.

Pilchards are used quite a lot along the coastline of Devon and Cornwall, while many anglers anoint their baits with pilchard oil. Frankly I have never had much luck with baits so anointed and feel that it is more or less one of those little superstitions of which there are no end in angling. However, the flesh of a pilchard is good for cod, haddock, mackerel and whiting.

Prawns can be obtained from a fishmonger, but are not such good baits as when obtained fresh from the sea. A live prawn is one of the best baits known for bass and pollack and is quite useful when used for mullet and flounders.

Sand-Eels, these are good for most fish. They can be used as live bait, for spinning when dead and what is more can be preserved in jars for use in the winter when the job of bait collecting is a difficult one. They can be hooked through the lips or the muscle just ahead of the large dorsal (back) fin. A supply can be obtained by digging at the edge of the sand when the tide is at its lowest. They can be preserved in a strong solution of brine, formalin or spirits of wine.

Shrimps are prolific breeders. Almost everything that swims in the sea feeds on shrimps, so it is no wonder that they make good baits for all manner of fish. Used alive they are excellent for bass, mullet, pollack and flat fish. Cod and whiting are also partial to them in the autumn.

OTHER BAITS

There are numerous other natural baits including cuttle, squid, sprat, razor fish, and lampreys, but they are more difficult to obtain than those described.

BAITS (ARTIFICIAL)

Using this type of bait is more or less a specialised form of angling and the novice would be well advised to stick to

RUBBER SAND EELS

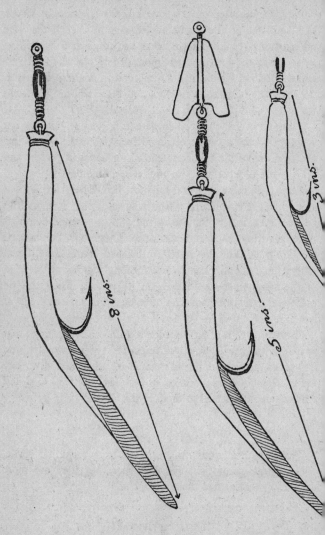

8 ins.

5 ins.

3 ins.

ARTIFICIAL BAITS

Rubber Ragworm

2¾ ins

Rubber Flexeel

2 ins

Soleskin

2¼ ins

Kidney Spoon

2½ ins

MACKEREL, BASS & POLLACK SPOONS

3in.

3½in.

3in.

natural bait for a time. Any good sea angler knows from experience that the best sport is obtained on natural bait, but on occasions the artificial will come into its own.

For the top and middle feeding fish spoons and silver and gold devons are good for use with a spinning rod. The mackerel, pollack and mullet can be taken on artificial fly, and also soleskin bait.

MACKEREL AND POLLACK FLY

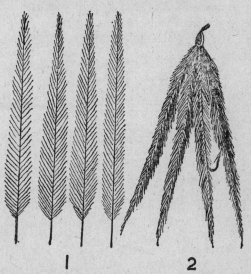

1. Four White Cock Hackle Feathers   2. Finished Fly

For bottom feeders there are several artificials made of rubber, such as the sand eel (various sizes and colours), mudworm and lugworm.

Of course there are numerous other artificials, but the ones mentioned have stood the test of time and where the water is 15 or 20 fathoms deep or even deeper the rubber sand-eel is good for cod, pollack and coalfish. Quite a large number of really large fish have fallen to the lure of the twisting rubber eel. When you do embark on artificial bait fishing do not be surprised if at first you fail to stir a fish to attack; persevere and some day the results will surprise you. The ranks of artificial bait casters will never be overcrowded.

In recent years a new artificial bait has made its appearance among sea angling baits. It is the plug bait which originated in the U.S.A. A jointed four inch plug worked deep is a very deadly bait for hake, cod and ling and when a shoal of bass or mackerel has been located a surface plug will provide quite a bit of fun.

CHAPTER IV

TIDE AND KNOT KNOWLEDGE

That the ebbing and flowing of the tides depend on solar and lunar influence there can be no doubt, for at every new and full moon we have high tides, while at half moon the tides are low.

In this corner of the globe (the British Isles) the tides are divided into two classes, the Neap Tide during which the movement of the water is small and the Spring Tide when the water movement is great.

It is common knowledge among professional anglers that there are few fishes which feed inshore or inside waters (estuaries) that are not directly influenced by the tides. Quite a number of species exhibit the greatest activity during the incoming tide while others are active in their search for food on the outgoing tide and during "slack water" between tides, therefore a little knowledge on this subject is useful at all times.

In the Spring the tides are high. This is caused by the sun and moon acting upon the earth in one and the same direction.

On the other hand, when the moon has completed her first and third quarter the attractive power at these points in her course is exercised at right angles to that of the sun, thus, preventing the waters from rising as high as before the neap or lower tides take place.

Many fishermen fish by the tides, but never really understand them.

As the tide comes up and gradually gains on the beach many kinds of fish come inshore to partake of the feast which is "unearthed" from the sand in the form of sand eels, lugworms, mudworms, and crustaceans. It is during this phase that the beach or surf angler as he is sometimes called comes into his own. For this kind of fishing the best sport is usually had during the Spring Tides because the water is stronger and this results in a greater dislodgement of sand and shingle. From my observations it appears that the feeding periods of most fish follow more closely the movement of the water in and out and not its actual rise and fall.

In Spring Tides boat fishing is not so good as many of the best spots are unfishable owing to the power of the waves. Neap Tides are generally best for fishing from a boat.

Newspapers published in coastal areas usually carry tides information, as do many almanacs, but in the event of such information not being available it is an easy matter to obtain it from the locals such as coastguards, professional fisherman or boatmen. Yet another method is to work them out for yourself and arrange your fishing accordingly. For instance the first thing is to find the age of the moon. The Spring Tides commence two tides before the new and full moon and continue for four days after. The Neap Tides commence with the second tide preceding the first and last quarters of the moon, the slackest being in the third tide. The Neap Tides end sixty hours later therefore the period between the highest tide and the lowest is roughly eight days.

The tides affect the currents and it is usual to find that they are strongest after the full moon.

The biggest storms usually occur during the Spring tides therefore it is a wise precaution when out with a boat to keep to windward and keep close to the shore. Never fish to leeward unless you are in a powered boat and accompanied by an expert sailor or you may find yourself swimming back, that is providing you can swim.

If at any time while fishing from a boat you should observe a heavy, dark troubled water line, advancing upon the water, it will be a coming squall and the quicker you reach shore the better.

A CEASELESS WAR

While on this question of tides and currents it is interesting to note that the ceaseless war raged against our shores by the sea has resulted in many new fishing grounds being made. Wherever erosion takes place there will be found fishing above the average, but while anglers have rejoiced, engineers and scientists have become alarmed at the erosion which is going on all round our shores. At the present time erosion is taking place all along the south coast. Hundreds of millions of tons of sand and shingle have been carried out to sea, though it is only occasionally, when the voracious sea takes an extra large mouthful that attention is called to the fact.

The sea is not particular as to where it bites. Right round the coast, from Durham, down the coasts of Yorkshire, Lincolnshire, Norfolk, Essex, Sussex, Kent, and up the Western coast to Cheshire and Lancashire, the erosion goes on. Off the north coast of Wales is a large tract of submerged land, now known as Lavan Sands and here I have had good sport on more than one occasion. Lavan Sands in days long ago used to be a fertile plain.

While the sea eats away the coast line in some places it builds up at others. The changes thus made affect fish life in that they frequent the places where there is most food. Thus in some seasons fishing is good in a certain place one year and indifferent another, but on those coast lines where there is an abundance of sand is a good place for surf fishing because the sand is the home of much of the food upon which most of the inshore species of fish feed.

Shingle beaches are not so good for fish food and if you are surf fishing the bait has to be got well out to where the food is, this is where a coastal chart comes in handy for it will indicate rocks, sand, wrecks, etc., and wherever there is a plentiful supply of food, and places to hide, there the angler will find fish.

KNOTS

In all angling knots play a major part, and as salt water fish are generally larger than those of fresh water great care should be taken when tying knots as the strength of any tackle is always weakest at the knots.

The ideal knot for sea fishing has yet to be invented and until it is we shall have to utilise the ones we have.

There are scores of different kinds, but only a few are used in actual fishing. Some knots are good for the job they have to do, others are not so good while others are almost useless. It does not necessarily follow that a knot because it is good for flax or braided or plaited nylon will answer in the case of monofilm. As a matter of fact experiments are still being carried out by the makers of this product and are likely to be for some time to come and until these experiments are successful the problem of knots will remain a problem.

One of the secrets of nylon's success is that unlike vegetable such as linen or cotton or animal fibres such as silk, it is a mineral fibre and cannot grow weak, or deteriorate with age.

Tie knots in nylon carefully and you will have no trouble. Where the friction is against any other material than nylon itself the knot tends to slip. Thus while hitch knots are good for silk, linen and cotton they are useless for nylon. In any kind of knot in which the friction is largely on the turns of the material itself there is no tendency to slip or untie.

I appreciate that it is a dangerous thing to attempt to lay down hard and fast rules about anything related to the sport of fishing. It's been tried many times, always with embarrassing repercussions. However, the knots now described are in common use among anglers and for my part until better ones are invented I shall use them.

For fastening an eyed hook to the terminal tackle the

HALF BLOOD KNOT

TURLE KNOT

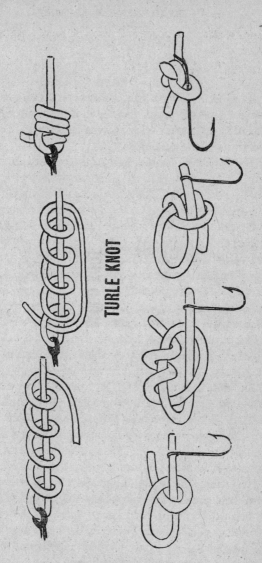

45

BIGHT KNOT

BLOOD KNOT

46

Four-turn Half Blood Knot is best. Put the end through the eye of the hook and place four turns round the main line. Next pass the end through the first turn made and pull tight and cut off any excess of the free end.

Another knot for fastening a hook to tackle is the *Turle*. Thread the hook and pass the end round the main line to form a loop, then make a couple of turns round the loop. The knot now looks like that in the third sketch and to complete it push the hook and tackle end through the loop and pull it tight.

For making a loop in line or terminal tackle the *Blood Bight* is as near perfect as any knot can be for the purpose for which it was designed. Make a loop at the end and twist it round as shown in the second sketch. In the third stage pass the single loop through the double one and pull tight and we have a knot that will stand up to a tremendous strain.

Our next is the *Blood* which at the moment is the best knot known for joining lengths of nylon together. In the first sketch we have two lengths to be united and in the second three turns have been taken and the end threaded down through the initial loop. In the third drawing three turns have been made at the other side of the initial loop and the end put up through the loop. All that remains now is to pull tight and cut off the ends close to the knot.

As I mentioned earlier on there are scores of knots, but if the novice will practice until he can tie one of the four described in the dark he need not bother about the others.

CHAPTER V

ROCK, PIER AND BEACH FISHING

And now that we have got through most of the technical details of tackle, etc., let us deal with the problems that attend the actual fishing. Most of us usually make a start from the rocks, pier or beach so we will look at that section of the sport first.

In fishing from rocks it is usual to find a good depth of water close inshore due to the shelving beach, therefore long casts are not necessary. In casting with a free-running Nottingham type reel the paternoster or ledger should be reeled in to about three inches from the end of the rod. Grip the rod with both hands – the right above the reel and the left below with the left hand thumb resting on the rim of the reel drum to prevent it from turning. Raise the rod above the head and lower the point until the whole rod is in a horizontal position, bring the rod smartly forward at the same time lifting the thumb from the reel. The bait will travel upward and forward in the direction in which the rod points. Just before the bait touches the water the thumb is again used as a slight brake on the reel thus preventing the line from becoming entangled with the reel, commonly known as an over-run or a bird's nest.

The timing of the thumb action both in releasing the line and braking the reel takes a bit of practice, but once the knack has been acquired very long distances can be cast quite easily. Incidentally this cast, the *Overhead*, is the best to use when fishing from a pier as there is little danger of hooking a passer-by.

The *Side Cast* is dangerous to use from a pier, but is perfectly safe if there is plenty of elbow room. The distance reached, however, is not so great as the overhead. It is just as simple to execute. Grasp the rod as before, but instead of putting it above the head hold it at a 45 degree angle in front facing the sea. Turn to the right as far as your hips will allow you, then swing back into your former position at the same time releasing the thumb from the reel drum and the power imparted to the rod will carry the bait out. While a little muscular energy is expended from the shoulders the main driving force is derived from the wrists. As in golf it is the swing and the timing, and in this only practice will make you expert. Multiplying reels are just as easy to use.

STANCE IS ALL IMPORTANT

A good stance is important and non-slip shoes will help in this respect when rock fishing. Some years ago I was in the Lake District and purchased a pair of climbing boots. Their steel-studded bottom and thick, soft leather uppers make ideal footwear for clambering over rocks and ensures a good foothold when casting. This type of fishing is fraught with many dangers unless your footwear is correct. Many anglers wear rubber wellingtons, but while they keep you dry they are not fool-proof when standing on glass-smooth, or wet and greasy rocks.

While such natural baits as lug and ragworms, crustaceans and fish flesh are good the rock angler can also get good sport with artificials such as the rubber sand eel and rubber ragworm for wherever there is an abundance of submerged rocks and a good depth of water one can expect to contact pollack, coalfish and conger. The first two will put up a good fight on light tackle, but with the conger it is a question of staying power. A favourite trick of this salt water eel is to wrap his tail round a rock or other convenient obstacle on feeling the pull of the hook and believe me the tackle has to be pretty strong to withstand the strain. Therefore when fishing where conger abound a wire trace is advisable for their teeth will sever the strongest nylon.

THE HIGHSPOT

Another fish which is partial to a rubber sand eel is the bass. This fish often breaks water by leaping into the air in its efforts to dislodge the hook and the fight throughout is not unlike that of a salmon. To me bass fishing is the high spot of all sea angling.

SANDY LANES

In some places float fishing can be quite profitable in the little bays formed by ridges of rocks and for this it is a good plan to take a walk during low tide at the spots one is thinking of fishing, during which a mental catalogue is made of the places most likely to be frequented by fish when the tide is in. A sandy lane between rocks is a good spot, but the cast must be accurate and care exercised when retrieving the tackle.

PROSPECTING

On one occasion I was fishing at Land's End in such a spot. For three hundred yards along the coast runs a strange formation. A hundred-foot cliff down to the water, and then a sort of shelf a dozen yards across and just an inch or two above the level of the sea. It is cut by a narrow chasm, always full of water and when the tide is in the ledge is under water. At low water it is possible with care to clamber all over the ledge.

The water is exceedingly clear below the ledge and with

the tide out it is possible to see down to the sea bed, a distance of several feet, and watch the teeming, fantastic sea life; delicately coloured sea-ferns, rose-tinted seaweeds and great purple sea-shrubs, which wave their branches continually as though some strong wind is blowing down there.

On the day this place was discovered I was out prospecting. As I peered over the ledge there was a flash of silver which shot out from under one of the purple shrubs and a bass dashed after a small fish, caught it and sank lazily back to his shelter to digest his morsel. There seemed to be quite a good number congregated below the ledge, in the sandy lane between another ridge of rocks.

VIRGIN SEA

Returning to my caravan I collected some tackle. I never saw such fishing! It was virgin sea, but before I could master casting the bait so that it was suspended by the float over the lane my supply of tackle had been reduced by three pater-nosters and two floats. However, by reducing the hooks to one and using a small float the problem was solved.

The fish had a positive preference for small shrimps and of course they were duly punished for it.

The next morning I had reached the rocks before the dawn had begun to break. It was too dark to fish; but I crept out to the very edge of the ledge, and sat down beside a great boulder to wait for the light. I lit a cigarette and smoked impatiently. It seemed as though the dawn came up out of the water itself; as the waves began to change colour from the dark, oily olive tint of night to a lighter green I put up my spinning rod and for the next two hours had excellent sport among bass and pollack who seemed to prefer a deeply worked gold devon to a more palatable and natural food.

My only object in relating the above is to show what can be done by a little prospecting before starting to fish.

FINDING FISH

The rules for finding fish are amazingly simple. A chat with local anglers is always good strategy, because living in the area they are fully aware of the changing conditions. If unable to contact a local angler there are signs at low water for the observant fisherman. For instance those spots along the shore where the action of the tide has washed out a basin, or undercut the rocks are always worth a trial at high water. Invariably they become tenanted with fish searching for food among the masses of seaweed.

Yet another is the large masses of floating seaweed. Fish always congregate around these for the titbits they contain such as shrimps, prawns, crabs, etc. Where such masses are seen and where there are rocks, there are always plenty of fish; the bait should be a shrimp or prawn. It is quite good fun float fishing under such conditions.

HAVE A LOOK AROUND

All round our coasts are places to delight the rock fisher, but the best sport will always reward the man who spends a little time looking around before settling to fish. The obvious spots should be ignored, for they will have been fished over dozens of times before, until a proper check has been made throughout the area.

Although there are thousands of sea anglers there's still a lot of virgin territory left in the salt water around our coasts, but it's up to *you* to find it. It may take some time and quite a number of trips, but when you do locate it you're in for a fishing thrill of a lifetime. And then remember – take all you need, but release the rest.

STATIONS AND BAITS

Round England the South and West coasts hold the

majority of good places, but to keep things in order we will start from the North-East and work our way round.

NORTHUMBERLAND: Craster, Whitley Bay and Monkseaton. *Fish* that can be expected are whiting, gurnard, pollack, codling, mackerel with occasional plaice. *Baits (natural)*; Lugworm, mussel, soft crab, mackerel or herring flesh. *Artificial:* Spoon, devon, and rubber sand-eel.

YORKSHIRE: Bridlington, Flamborough and Scarborough. *Fish*: Coalfish, pollack, whiting, gurnard, mackerel, plaice, with occasional cod. *Baits (natural):* Lugworm, mussel, shrimp, prawn, mackerel flesh and sand-eel. *Artificial:* Rubber sand-eel and ragworm, spoon and devon.

KENT: Margate, Sandgate, and Hythe. *Fish:* Bass, codling, plaice, pouting. *Baits (natural):* Lug and ragworm, mussel, shrimp, crab and squid. *Artificial:* Rubber sand-eel and ragworm.

DEVON: Brixham, Dartmouth, and Plymouth. *Fish*: Bass, dab, bream, pouting, mackerel and occasional wrasse. *Baits (natural):* Pilchard, mussel, crab, shrimp, prawn, razor fish, squid, sand-eel and lugworm. *Artificial*: Rubber sand-eel, spoon and devon.

CORNWALL: This in my opinion is the best bit of coastline for the rock angler as there are more species feeding close in than anywhere else. Goran Haven, Looe, Porthleven, Newquay, Penzance and Land's End. *Fish:* Bass, mackerel, pollack, coalfish, wrasse, plaice, bream, ling, whiting and pouting. *Baits (natural):* Sand-eel, mussel, pilchard, crab, shrimp, prawn, lugworm and mackerel and herring flesh soaked in pilchard oil. *Artificial:* Rubber sand-eel, spoon, devon and plug.

WALES: There are only a few good places for rock fishing round this coast line and furthermore the fish do not run to a large size.

SCOTLAND: Port Patrick, Stranraer, Port Appin, Shieldaig, Loch Torridon, Gairloch and Cape Wrath. Of course there

are scores of other places for rock fishing but so far the author has not had a chance to visit them, but as a guide I would say that the coastline of Ross and Cromarty and Sutherland would be best for prospecting, but a car for transport is essential. *Fish:* Haddock, whiting, plaice, sole, pollack, coalfish and cod are the fish most likely to be met with. *Baits (natural):* Mussel, sand-eel, crab, prawn, shrimp, mackerel and herring flesh. *Artificial:* Rubber sand-eel and spoon. By the way take my advice, don't fish on a Sunday in Scotland, it is considered very bad taste.

ISLE OF MAN: There are numerous places around this lovely island to delight the rock angler. *Fish:* Pollack, whiting, plaice, haddock, and mackerel. *Baits:* Mussel, lug and ragworm, shrimp, crab, mackerel and herring flesh. *Artificial:* Rubber sand-eel, devon and plug.

IRELAND: The whole length of the west coast abounds with good rock fishing possibilities. A car is advisable as transport is none too good. *Fish:* all the species found round the English coasts with the exception of bass which are not plentiful. *Baits (natural):* Sand-eel, soft crab, prawn, shrimp, mussel and mackerel and herring flesh.

BEST TIMES

In regard to the various species the best seasons are: *Bass:* Summer and Autumn. *Cod and Codling:* Autumn and Winter. *Coalfish:* Summer and Autumn. *Dab:* Summer and Autumn. *Gurnard:* Summer and Autumn. *Mackerel:* Summer and Autumn. *Plaice:* Summer and Autumn. *Pollack:* Practically the whole year. *Pouting:* Whole year. *Whiting:* Summer, Autumn and Winter. *Wrasse:* Summer.

FROM THE PIER

In fishing from piers and jetties one can expect to be a little crowded for space and the only possible way of securing a good position is to be up early. Many anglers use a couple of rods, one for float work and the other for ledgering or fishing the paternoster. For my part one is sufficient as with two you are bound to divide your attention, often at the moment when your concentration is most needed.

Around most piers and jetties there is always a good depth of water which is inhabited by quite a few fish. They are constantly on the watch for their enemies or any movement between themselves and the light. They would, therefore, be more likely to see a bait that is above them than one that is on the bottom. Of course on occasions most fish that reside inshore around piers and jetties often go "grubbing" among the foundations for food and it is then that a ledger will be found quite good. These occasions normally coincide with very low water.

At high water and also when the tide is on the turn the fish mostly keep off the bottom. Float fishing with a light paternoster is just the thing, for should you have fished deep without success you can rise the baits a foot at a time until you are rewarded. This is done by shortening the weight tackle and for this purpose strong nylon is most suitable, but taking it all round it is one of those things with which experiments must be made.

The use of heavy weights is often very unsatisfactory as it puts too much of a strain on rods and when a fish is hooked there is little sport because of the weight. In boat fishing such weights are a necessity due to the depths one has to go, but this is not the case when fishing from piers and jetties. It is rare that long casts are needed as the fish invariably congregate around the pier.

The feeding habits of fish are very unpredictable. Some days they will strike every kind of natural bait and artificial you may offer them and on the other hand, there are days they will look upon the most choice bait with disgust. To be able to take fish constantly under all conditions is a feat that very few expert anglers accomplish.

There are three major periods during a day to catch fish and while early morning and later afternoon are excellent, an hour before and up to the top of high tide is considered one of the very best times.

Skate, conger, bass, mackerel and mullet have all been taken by pier fishermen in the south and west, but on the east coast anglers have quite a lot of sport with whiting, gurnard, pollack and coalfish.

BASS

For bass, live prawns and shrimps are good, with a sand-eel excellent. Keep your baits near the piles and stanchions of the pier as the waves start to roll in with the tide. From the last week in April to the end of August is the best time to pier fish for this salt-water scrapper.

At high tide a spinning rod is worth a try. The artificial should be a gold or silver devon and it should not be worked too deep.

It is also possible to take bass on the fly rod, but this is a specialist form of sport. I have fly-fished for them on numerous occasions but have yet to register a kill, yet a friend of mine swears by this method. The fly he uses is a large Alexandra dressed on a No. 4 salmon hook.

MACKEREL

Should you be on the pier and notice a large flock of gulls wheeling and diving into the water it is a sure sign that mackerel are about. There is no surer way to locate feeding mackerel than by first spotting feeding gulls and if you can get your bait into the area the results will be fast and packed with plenty of thrills.

This streamlined distant cousin of the mighty tunny likes company and so they move around in schools feeding on the young of other fish, and what they don't eat in their slashing attacks the gulls usually do.

For this kind of fishing the spinning rod is the best tool and the bait a mackerel lask (see illustration, page 34) properly weighted can be cast long distances. Reel in moderately fast and if you are fortunate enough to place your bait in the feeding zone sport is almost assured. So long as the gulls continue their screaming and diving you can be sure the fish are round about, but once the gulls move off or float lazily on the water it is a definite sign that the mackerel have gone.

Mid-summer and early autumn are the best times for this kind of fishing for then the mackerel are working along the shore-line in their search for fish fry.

CONGER EEL

Should there be any wrecks or large ridges of rock in the near vicinity of the pier it is a safe bet that a conger or two have taken up residence. Strong tackle and a good rod and reel are needed for these fellows and a gaff to land them is a necessity. Squid is a good bait, but difficult to obtain, but excellent results have been achieved by anglers using a whole mackerel. The most important thing to remember in going after this sea eel is to be perfectly sure that the bait is fresh. Many fishermen with good equipment, plenty of patience and enthusiasm, miss catching a conger because they offer a stale bait. I have seen fishermen put a mackerel on the hook in the approved way, that is by taking out the backbone and binding the two halves on to the hook with tinned copper wire, and then wonder why they did not catch a fish. The answer was that they purchased the mackerel from a fish-monger who probably had had the fish in his frig' for several days. If you cannot catch your own bait the best way is to purchase a few from a professional fisherman, then you know it is fresh. There is no question of luck when one man succeeds alongside another angler who does not get a bite. The secret is bait freshness.

The bait should be about a yard from the weight so that it will be off the bottom. The trace should be wire to withstand the teeth of the conger when he joins battle with the angler.

SKATE

The rod, reel and tackle used for conger is also suitable for common skate fishing and here again a fresh mackerel makes a good bait. A gaff is needed because you never know when your opponent may be of large size. The larger species love very deep water and it is only on rare occasions that they have been recorded as being taken in shallow water such as one finds round piers and jetties.

GREY MULLET

The mullet at certain places on the south coast is a pier angler's fish and puts up a surprisingly good fight when taken on light tackle. His haunts will be round the stanchions of the pier so long casts are not necessary. The bait I have had most sport with is the ragworm and as the mullet's lips are very tender a small hook is much better than a large one. There is no need to use heavy tackle when after this fish as they do not run to great size. A four pound mullet is considered a good fish while a six or eight pounder is exceptional. One angler I know uses a roach rod and a four X cast. He gets quite a lot of fun out of his fishing.

The hooks I use range from No. 10 to No. 14 and while a ledger or a paternoster will at times take a few fish the best way is float fishing. The float can be the same as that when used in fishing for river roach and the shot on the cast should be placed in the same manner. Of course the number of shot will depend on the kind of water being fished and the size of float used.

The bite of a mullet is not unlike that of a roach and the angler's strike while firm should not be too strong. Early morning and late evening are the best times to go after this species.

Other baits recommended include uncooked fresh peeled prawns and shrimps and lugworm.

BEACH ANGLING

This method is without doubt just as interesting as the other two yet it is safe to say that it is the least understood. Many novices at the outset of their fishing career think that beach or surf fishing is simple and entails one thing, the capability of heaving a heavy lead above which is attached ledger or paternoster tackle. Nonsense. To be able to cast a long line is a very nice achievement, but it does not guarantee the capture of fish. On occasions long casts are necessary, but in the main, medium casts will be found to be most profitable.

As I mentioned previously the rod should be strong without being like a broom handle, stiff but pliant enough to stand up to the strain of casting six ounce or eight ounce weights. An aged Cornish beach fisherman long since passed on, told me some years ago that in this type of fishing the best chance of success is to get the bait out a distance of 25 to 30 yards from the edge of the water on the beach. Yet another angling friend believes that if he can place his bait behind the third incoming roller (wave) he has a good chance of connecting with a foraging fish. Both methods are commendable. Some anglers throw their bait out as far as they can and as the tide rises they shift their rod back, thus at high tide their bait might be anything from 80 to 120 yards away. I have seen several good bass taken this way, the last occasion was at Bournemouth. The angler in question had fished all day without success from the pier and then towards evening he changed his tackle and went on to the beach and in less than an hour had captured three nice bass, the largest being a three pounder.

Drift-lining is also good when the tide is advancing. For this method a No. 4 hook is advisable to which is fastened a generous piece of fresh mackerel. The trace should be strong nylon and the only weight needed is three or four small split shot. Cast well out into the waves whose action will keep it on the move backwards and forwards. I have used this quite successfully when bass have been about. Flounders and plaice often succumb to the drift-line.

KEEP FEET DRY

For surf fishing it is advisable to wear thigh boots, frankly I know of nothing more miserable than fishing in wet feet, particularly in the cool of the evening. It is the surest way of catching a cold, and so having a poor holiday, that I know.

The rod should be equipped with a spear so that it can be fixed in the sand with ease to lean against the rod-rest at an angle of about 45 degrees. A bell clipped to the rod top is also very useful, for while the movement of the waves and undertow rarely ring the bell the sharp tug of a hooked fish will.

STUDY THE BEACH

If the beach you are fishing is shingle then the fish you can expect is bass and in the autumn and winter, cod, but should it be sand, bass, flatfish, and mullet might be taken.

Two or three hook paternosters are the tackles mostly used and the baits can be lugworm, shrimp, prawn or mackerel flesh. If you are fishing near an estuary the best baits will be ragworm and sand-eel.

A shelving beach like that at Dungeness offers most scope, for the simple reason that there is always a greater depth of water and consequently more food.

On those beaches, where the sand extends well out into the sea at low tide, flounder fishing can be a good proposition and what is more can be most enjoyable for the juvenile angler. The fish will be mostly on the small side ranging from four ounces to eight ounces.

It is a pleasant way of whiling away the time in between the tides. Here's how. Walk to the edge of the water and cast well out. Let the baits, lugworms on a two hook ledger, lie for about ten minutes and then reel in slowly, very slowly over the sand. As the baits are brought forward their progress will disturb the fine sand, just the same as a live lugworm would do when in the act of burrowing. It is this displacement of sand along the trails of the baits that attracts the flounders and what is more if there are any plaice about they will also be interested. A weight of no more than two ounces is ample for this sort of work.

If lugworms are not available, mussels, live shrimps and small prawns will answer quite well.

Plaice love those sandy beaches where there are bays and any beach so formed is worth prospecting for these delightful table fish. Lugworm or mussel are two of the best baits known.

Flounders and also plaice are not vicious biters and to detect a bite it is advisable to use the lightest line possible as it offers the least resistance to the waves.

BEWARE OF THE WEAVER

Fishing in sandy places is not without danger to the angler. Inhabiting such spots is the weaver, a fish well able to take care of itself. At the back of its head is a crest with five spines which are very poisonous. There are also a number of smaller spines on the gill covers which are also poisonous. Along the south coast it is fairly common and has earned the unwelcome title of "viper fish".

For the beginner it is important that he should be able to recognize this menace so that he can cut his line without touching it, because, believe me, the weaver's sting is not to be trifled with. Several deaths have been recorded from such poisoning.

Fortunately it is an easy matter to identify the weaver. I have seen many weavers and they have all ranged in size from six to eight inches although I have heard of larger ones being caught. Here's how to recognize this peril. Behind the spiny crest is a long dorsal fin, the tail is concave and covering the body from the gill covers are a series of diagonal lines which continue to the tail. Dark brown in colour it is these markings which identifies this fish. So should you be unfortunate enough to hook one take my advice and cut it loose, don't take a chance for it isn't worth it. Should you be unlucky enough to get stung apply Scrubb's Ammonia to the wound as quickly as possible.

Even without fish there is something fascinating about a beach when the tide is coming in, at least I have always found it so. The sea rumbles up and along the beach, rises in a tall curve and breaks with the sound of a muffled drum; sand trickles forward to be scooped up, to be folded and kneaded and rolled; and a long diminishing sigh encircles all. Its blues and greens are drawn, like its gold, from the sky; gulls wheel and dip in counterpoint, and from behind a curved screen of colour the moon moves it in a rhythm in which we too have part, so that in the sea's presence we find release, a common being, and are at one.

IN DETAIL

Good places for pier or beach fishing include the following:
NORTHUMBERLAND: Alnmouth, Craster, Whitley Bay. *Fish* to

be expected are pollack, codling and flounder. *Baits:* as previously mentioned.

YORKSHIRE: Bridlington good from both pier and beach. *Fish:* Dabs, whiting, coalfish and codling.

NORFOLK: Yarmouth provides fairly regular sport from pier and beach. *Fish:* Dabs, flounders, whiting and codling.

SUFFOLK: Lowestoft from pier and beach. *Fish:* Dabs, flounders, plaice and whiting.

ESSEX: Clacton, Southend-on-Sea, each has pier and beach fishing which in the late summer is really good. *Fish:* Dabs, flounders, bass and mullet.

KENT: Herne Bay, Margate, Dungeness. In the case of the first named the fishing from both pier and beach is among the best in the country while at Dungeness the shelving beach ensures excellent sport. *Fish:* Conger, codling, dabs, flounders, plaice, pouting and mackerel.

SUSSEX: Hastings, best fishing is from pier. *Fish:* Bass, plaice, codling and whiting.

HANTS.: Bournemouth, good in spring and late summer and autumn from both pier and beach. *Fish:* Bass, grey mullet, dabs, codling and plaice.

DORSET: Lyme Regis at times excellent beach fishing. *Fish:* Bass and Mackerel.

DEVON: Torquay, Plymouth and Dartmouth. The first two have pier and beach fishing which is excellent. *Fish:* Pollack, dabs, mackerel, bass and occasional bream and mullet.

CORNWALL: Looe, Goran Haven, Polperro and Penzance. *Fish:* Pollack, conger, whiting, bass and occasional bream.

PEMBROKE: Tenby, excellent from pier and beach. *Fish:* Bass, whiting and pollack with occasional codling.

CARNARVON: Penmaenmawr. *Fish:* Dabs, whiting and codling with occasional mackerel.

SCOTLAND: Right down the whole west coast is good and it would be a difficult job to pick out the best. *Fish:* As already mentioned for rock fishing.

ISLE OF MAN: Douglas, Peel, Port Erin, and Ramsay all excellent. *Fish:* Pollack, wrasse, mackerel, ling, haddock, dabs and flounders.

IRELAND: Right down the south coast is excellent, the best being situated between Kilmore Quay in County Wexford and Valentia in County Kerry. The west coast is good in many places, but accommodation and transport are none too good.

A good idea is to hire a car and take a tent and provisions with you.

CHAPTER VI

BOAT FISHING

The search for buried treasure always gives a thrill and what hidden treasure could be more priceless to an angler than the locating of a fishing spot (known among sea anglers as a mark) as near virgin as makes no matter.

One of the beauties of this type of fishing is that the angler is practically free to roam as he will and in his wanderings it is almost certain that he will sooner or later enjoy some of his finest sport with rod and line. I may add that intelligent and trustworthy observations are at all times of value and that in addition to its many other charms boat fishing may fairly be said to be a directly instructive and intellectual pleasure. Each successive fact that is stored up in the memory opening out yet another to the searching mind and serving to prevent a captivating sport from degenerating into a mere fish-hunting pursuit.

While good sport can be had from pier, beach or rocks, for the man who is intent on giving battle to the larger species a boat is the answer. He will be able to get in touch with huge skate, conger, pollack, tope, etc., and in addition he will be assured of better sport among the mackerel and bass.

WATCH THE BIRDS

From a boat one uses a bottom rod, fly rod or spinning rod as the occasion demands. As in beach fishing the actions of the sea birds point to good fishing amongst those gamesters the mackerel and bass. When the birds circle compactly and dive into the water you can be sure there are one or other of the species mentioned in the area. If it is a school of mackerel that is responsible for the commotion, let the boat drift into the school and put the fly rod to work.

What flies? Mackerel are not particular in their choice of patterns, but the angler has to bear in mind two things, how and where the fly is fished, for these are much more important than its shape, size or colour. I have taken quite a number of mackerel on a large Alexandra fly, the colour combination of which is green, red and silver, but in general practice combinations of red, white and yellow will answer quite well. That is what I like about mackerel, they are not fussy. Your fly is cast into a school and retrieved slowly and in a matter of minutes you are fighting one of these streamlined beauties. Although never very large (average one pound) their fight for freedom is thrilling. With the spinning rod a mackerel lask can be cast long distances and quite often it will be found to be more deadly than the fly. No doubt because as it moves in the water it is not unlike the small fish the mackerel are feeding on.

For the bass, once a school has been found, devons, spoons and small rubber sand-eels will provide sport, and while the fight of a mackerel is fast and furious that of a bass can be a long drawn out affair, a game of give and take.

With small boats (rowing) it is always advisable to fish at such times and places as will enable you to make sure of assistance from the tide when homeward bound. With a powered boat there is no such worry.

EMPLOY A BOATMAN

For the novice it is best to employ a boatman or contract to go with a professional fisherman, for then all there is to think about is fishing.

However, we will assume that you are going to take out a boat. The first thing to do is to purchase an Admiralty chart of the area, these can be purchased in most coastal towns. On some charts I have had, the soundings are given in feet and on others in fathoms, why the difference I do not know.

Before you rent the boat look it over. Make sure there is a baler just in case you ship some water and see that the oars are in good condition. A damaged or badly patched oar can be a menace, remember they are your means of locomotion therefore a few minutes spent in examining them is not wasted. Next check the anchor rope to see that it is not frayed to danger point. Most boat proprietors check their boats every day and periodically they are examined by an inspector, but it is always better to be on the safe side.

In the autumn fogs are pretty frequent and for the venturesome angler who likes to fish well out at sea a compass is a necessity, for having taken a reading when the anchor is let down it is an easy matter to reach the landing stage in a fog. One thing to remember in taking a compass reading, move all metal articles out of the way first or the reading will be a false one. Even a wristlet watch or a ring will create a deflection in the needle.

For any angler who likes deep water work, the purchase of a good compass is an investment. With it one can return to the same spot day after day and what is more in conjunction with the chart all the best spots can be explored to a yard or two. A compass takes up very little room and to use an old and worn cliche, it is worth its weight in gold.

Of course it is understood that an open boat is not for the individual who lacks knowledge of boat management. For those who are unaware of the treacherous moods of the sea I repeat – employ a boatman.

FOR YOUR FEET

As to clothing a good pair of boots is preferable to wellingtons or thigh boots. For one thing boots give a better grip on wet planking and should you be capsized it is only a few seconds job to kick off a pair of boots whereas taking off thigh boots or wellingtons can be a long task and they might easily prove fatal to the wearer under such conditions. Always see that your boots are fastened with knots easy to undo just in case of accidents, for with the sea you never can tell and it is a wise man who anticipates the worst.

An oil-skin coat is useful in case of a sudden squall, while in the tackle bag there should be a good sized cloth for handling such spiny fish as bass, gurnard, etc.

As to the tackle required for boat fishing that has already been dealt with in a previous chapter.

Once you have decided on the boat make up your mind as to what type of fish you want to go after and in this you will be greatly assisted by the chart.

Take a goodly assortment of natural baits and also artificials. Never put lug and ragworms together as one kills the other and to keep sand-eels alive you will need a wicker basket, known among anglers as a courge. In this container prawns and sand-eels can be placed and towed behind the boat.

Place your tackle near to hand so as to prevent having to stretch or stand up to reach it. Standing up in a rowing boat is a very dangerous thing to do when you are on your own as it upsets the trim of the boat and with no passengers to counterbalance your changed position you are liable to capsize.

In your tackle always include a net and gaff. Netting or gaffing a fish from a boat can be a difficult job. One reason why there are failures is that the angler has not judged aright the length of line to have out.

Usually netting is harder than gaffing. Properly played a fish does not feel the gaff until the stroke is completed. But in the case of the net there is the danger that the fish may touch the rim and then in all probability he begins a fresh struggle for freedom.

The net should be sunk and the fish brought over it. All that remains is to lift and the fish is in the net. Never let a fish go in tail first, for so netted it may easily gain its freedom by jumping out.

MAKE A FINAL CHECK

Before leaving the shore see that you have all your equipment and tackle safely stowed away. In your pockets there should be a good knife, small roll of adhesive tape and iodine. The last two named articles are for personal use in case of accidents with hooks or spines of fish.

Frankly I prefer fishing by myself, but that pleasure only came after I had served a long and arduous apprenticeship in overcrowded motor-boats and uncomfortable three and four man rowing boats. In this type of fishing, however, one makes many friends.

When a young man, I experienced my first taste of boat-fishing off the coast of Northumberland, my companions were good boatmen and as the result of that outing there was born a desire to master the difficult art of boat management.

The nimble fingers of dawn were busy in the east as we noiselessly glided away from the jetty at Craster. Doug, sitting in the stern makes three heaps of the cockles which he has gathered a few moments ago, standing knee-deep in the water while his skilled hands rummaged for them in the sand. The contents represent bait, and the first step in a subtle progression which ends in breakfast.

"Pull on the left!" is his murmured warning to Tom, whose oar deftly steers the boat round the jetty, disturbing a seagull which flaps lazily off duty – the last sentinel of night.

"Looks fat and well-fed," is the oars-man's comment; Doug's answering, "Aye", concludes their way of saying that it has been a good fishing spring. Shy silent men, these, who harmonize simply into their surroundings. Doug knows all there is to know of the fish of these waters: their habits, their favourite haunts and their fancies in regard to diet. His bait-tin, malodorous though it is to me, contains titbits that tempt alike the pollack and mackerel of the upper levels, or the cod, whiting, haddock and the various species of flat fish in the depths below. Such matters have been his study since boyhood in the district, and it is a deep knowledge that prompts his broad, tolerant grin for those be-flannelled tourists who at unlikely times visit this little Northumberian fishing village and tangle their tackle at the jetty's end.

"Sure the fish know them," he says, "and enjoy their visits."

Tom chuckles about them, too, for being only in the sea anglers' "B" grade himself he has much sympathy for their vagaries.

Doug steps carefully over his lowered oar-handle to the nose of the boat, and lets down the anchor. This is pollack ground, and before we can tempt the creatures near the sea bed we must have pollack or mackerel for bait. This is the reason that three cockle-laden hooks flip overboard, pivoted into position by floats which allow them to dangle a dozen feet below the surface, where the pollack play among the rocks. This is the reason why we sit – three men in a boat – in a kingdom of silence; a silence broken only by the tip-tap of the waves below our gunwhale, or the distant mournful cry of a seagull.

There are two outstanding impressions that one always carries away from Craster. First, that it is steeped in silence; second, that the silence is an attribute of the great age which broods over it. Age speaks in the fretted cliffs on which the village is perched and which fringe the water.

Even the two men beside me seem to fit into the picture – Tom nonchalantly idling over the boat side; Doug sitting straighter, the line running taut over his index finger.

Suddenly this moves, as upon a trigger; the other hand comes swiftly into play, and in a flash two glistening pollack are thrown into the boat. "A double! Must be hungry," is his only remark.

Then a new plan of campaign develops. The still wriggling bodies are beheaded, gutted and filleted, and soon four ounce leads carry our hand-lines with new baits into the 25 fathom below.

"Everything's hungry," laughs Tom good-naturedly, as he pulls up his paternoster with two naked hooks. A sharp tug and run brings me back to the business in hand, and it isn't very long before a contest between human skill and natural cunning ends in my bringing inboard a 5-lb pollack. In half an hour Doug has four and Tom and I two each.

By this time the sun was climbing steadily into a cloudless sky, so I got out my spinning rod and tackle and prepared to try conclusions with the mackerel which were becoming active as indicated by the frenzied flying and contortions of the hundreds of gulls.

The bait I used (an artificial) was a $1\frac{1}{2}$-inch silver and gold spoon. However, I soon discovered that the pollack were more interested in the spoon than the mackerel, and it was over an hour before I boated one. After that they came quickly and by the time we were ready to lift anchor to go in for breakfast my score was twelve mackerel and nine pollack. So ended my initiation into boat fishing.

AN AMBITION

Following that expedition came others, but all the time I was longing for the day when I should consider myself proficient to take out a boat myself. Many years ago that opportunity came.

I had been to Cape Wrath on business and while there had hired a boatman at Sheigra, a few miles away, to take me out. On arrival at Sheigra I found my boatman was down with the 'flu so decided to take the boat out myself, if allowed to do so.

Do you know the Scottish coast opposite the Western Isles? It is a part of the British Isles where some of the finest sea fishing abounds if one is not afraid of loneliness. Little villages are tucked among the grey cliffs of gloomy headlands. The desolation of that countryside! Talk about the jumping-off place.

You hear of Scotland and you think of bagpipes and kilts and as a result I was not prepared for the bleakness of that landscape. Rocky pasturelands and treeless crags swept by salt spray and sky. Miles between villages where the coast roads climbed off into nowhere; lonely shepherd's cottages; dark glens echoing the boom of the surf; valleys forlorn with cold-running streams and ancient stone fences and here and there some sullen old building frowning down from a barren eminence.

It wasn't the Scotland I had pictured.

Like the countryside the natives were taciturn and morose. Frosty-faced old shepherds regarded me with suspicion and I might as well have talked to the flocks of sheep that imperviously blocked the roads.

However, at the end of three days we were all friends and of the fisherfolk I have nothing but praise for their kindness.

On the fourth day I was granted permission to take out the boat.

For a whole week I was captain and crew of that little cockle-shell and drank to the full the sweet, soft scent that comes from the sea. The sport was good, flat fish, whiting, pollack and coalfish were there in abundance just waiting it seemed for someone to come along and catch them. The tackle was a three hook paternoster, eight ounce weight and the reel a wooden Scarborough. Baits included mussel, crab and the flesh of other fish.

It is not until you take out a boat by yourself that you really understand the meaning of the word "*free*".

FOR THE ESTUARY

A boat is a great asset when estuary fishing for mullet, flounder and bass.

We will take the mullet first as it is one of our finest estuary-loving fish. As the season advances they move in and out of the estuaries with the tides. After selecting your spot drop the anchor and then throw in a little ground bait composed of soaked bread well mixed with bran. Wait about ten minutes then case out your tackle comprising float and No. 12 hook on which has been pressed a little of the ground bait. A piece about the size of a hazel nut is ideal. Do not let the line become taut, but have a yard or so lying slack in the rod rings and when the line begins to draw out quickly, strike.

To hook a mullet the strike must be made as the fish is swimming away for this species hold the bait in their mouths for quite a long time before swallowing. As a matter of fact it is a rare thing to catch one that has swallowed the hook. If the float goes under and then rises to the surface again the chances are you have lost the fish, only by the closest attention to the float can you hope to strike at the proper moment.

Never underestimate the mullet. It is strong, very fast when hooked, and the brain inside its well-shaped head is capable of figuring a way out of a lot of trouble, as professional fishermen often learn to their cost. On one occasion while fishing a Devon estuary a net fisherman told me that repeatedly he had lost large numbers of good mullet through their jumping out over the corks of the net.

On occasions during the summer months large shoals of mullet travel miles up estuaries and at such times their principal diet seems to be a weed that grows on sunken woodwork, such as piles, etc. Should you locate any you will most certainly find mullet. Put a little of the green slimy weed on the hook and fish it the same as paste.

Other good baits, when the fish are well up an estuary, include ordinary garden worms, ragworm, freshwater shrimp and caddis grub. I have had them take ordinary maggot and wasp grub, but not often.

AFTER DARK

In all estuary fishing, after dark will always produce better fish than during the daytime. It is my opinion that the really big fellows do most of their feeding at night. The warmer the weather the better chance you have of a four or five pounder. There's no way of knowing for certain at what hour fishing on a given night will hit its peak but, by and large, I have found most action with mullet around midnight and in the pre-dawn hours. Just one angler's experience; take it for what it's worth.

Fishing at night is just like fishing in the daytime except that you handle your tackle by touch alone. For safety's sake casting should be by the overhead method. On all but the blackest nights your eyes will find enough light to make out the shoreline. It helps a lot to know the water you're fishing therefore a slow walk along the bank during daylight should be made and any obstruction in the area you propose fishing should be noted. In night fishing a flashlight is a necessity, but don't wave it around any more than you have to.

Flounder fishing can provide quite a few thrills if light tackle is used. This lover of estuaries is not a spectacular fighter it is true, but he is a willing feeder and a delicacy in the frying pan. The flounder prefers a sandy bottom, sometimes he may be as small as a man's hand and on other occasions he will be quite large, two pounders are often caught in the autumn.

As the tide rises the water in the estuary is the time to go after these obliging flatfish. At low water take note where the sand flats are and in the evening as the tide is coming in anchor your boat just on the outskirts of the flat you have selected for your evening's work.

Ledgering is best with the lightest possible weight. The bite of a flounder is gentle, but once he takes hold he does not let go. The bait should rest lightly on the bottom so that the undertow of the tide, as it sweeps back and forth, moves it to and fro. As the movement of the tidal water churns up the sand out will come the flounders and if you have selected your spot with care you should not be long without a bite.

For this type of fishing the best baits are shrimp and mussel. Soft crab and lug and ragworms make a good second best if the other two are not available.

Baited spoon fishing is also an excellent method, the bait being a ragworm. The spoon is cast well out and reeled in slowly. When a bite is felt stop reeling for four or five seconds and usually by the end of that time the fish has the bait well in its mouth, when the strike can be made.

The *Bass* without a doubt provides more thrills for the boat angler who is not keen on the heavyweight species than any other fish known. It has often been called the poor man's salmon and in fighting ability he is not unlike that noble fish. On occasions some really good fish have been taken from pier and rocks, but to be fairly sure of landing a big one there is nothing to beat a boat. In the main the best bass fishing is off our southern and western coasts. It is not an easy fish to catch and care should be exercised in the assembling of the tackle to see that every part functions well. On occasions they feed near the surface and on others well down, but they do not like very deep water. In marks where the water is 20 to 30 fathoms the bait should not be lower than six to eight fathoms.

From a boat there is nothing to touch a live sand-eel, large bass tumble over each other to get at them, but for this method a companion is needed to row the boat slowly just off shore. This type of angling is called "slow railing" and when the tide is on the way in it can at times be very deadly. A live prawn, when sand-eels are not available can be used for "railing" but is more fragile to use.

When bass are feeding near the surface the spinning rod will take a few as will a fly rod, but for good sport always use live bait.

"Drift-lining" is another good way of taking a bass or two. In this the bait is allowed to drift with the tide just below the surface and to enable the angler to do this a reel capable of holding at least 200 yards of ten pound line should be used. Use only sufficient lead to stop the bait from coming to the surface. It is fatal to put on a weight that will carry the bait to the bottom for in the first place you will probably lose your tackle among rocks and other obstructions and secondly you will take very few bass.

In "drift-lining" the best time is when the tide is half-way to being high and continuing until it is midway to low tide.

DEEP-WATER FISHING

In fishing a mile or more off shore it is advisable to use a motor boat with a skilled boatman in charge. It is when one goes after leviathians of the deep that the cream of salt-water angling is tasted. You will not get the flashing runs of a bass or mackerel when battling a conger or skate, but there will be thrills galore before the gaff goes home.

There are many places round our coasts where good conger can be taken, but Ireland holds pride of place so far as skate is concerned, for hardly a season passes, but some lucky angler hands a hundred pounder.

Dungeness according to old records appears to be the best English conger station, the old record was set up there in

1933, and since then there have been several over 50-lb. taken.

The best times are mid-summer and throughout autumn and the best sport will be had when fishing at night. It is bottom fishing so tackle should be of the best. A medium-sized fish once he has his tail round a rock will make the angler think he is fastened to a wreck and not until there are some severe jerks to the rod top will he realise that a fish is hooked.

Bait freshness has already been mentioned and also the type of tackle necessary. Even when gaffed a conger can be an ugly customer and the best way of avoiding accidents is to get it into a large sack as quickly as possible, therefore when embarking on a conger expedition remember to take a sack along. Getting a conger in a sack can be a lengthy job due to the contortions of the fish, but the boatmen along the south coast are adept at it and also at killing them by severing the vertebra at the back of the head with a sharp knife. Until proficient at this art it is best to let your boatman do it. Another point worth remembering, never let your hands get too near the mouth of a conger. A friend of mine lost a thumb as a result of being too careless. Harness *must* be worn for big ones.

Skate fishing at least when you have hooked a big one is a tiring affair for the breadth of the fish enables it to hug the bottom as if it were glued there and the fight as a result, even with powerful tackle, can be a prolonged business. Valencia (Ireland) and also Ballycotton (Ireland) are where the largest specimens abound. For these monsters harness must be worn by the angler. Whole mackerel and herring are good baits for the larger species with lugworm, mussel and fish flesh admirable for the smaller ones, fish of thirty to sixty pounds.

The south coast is a favourite spot of mine when after small skate. A queer thing about this fish is that the "face" is very often grotesquely human in appearance.

Other fish which the boat angler will take include black and red bream, coalfish, pollack, cod, whiting, gurnard, haddock, hake, john dory, ling, plaice, tope, turbot and wrasse.

Black and *Red Bream* fishing usually starts in early summer and continues until late autumn. They range round our southern and western coastlines in shoals and while the former is looked upon as a sporting bottom fish the latter while being a good food fish can be a nuisance to the angler when after other species, due to its greedy habits.

Along the Sussex coast and off North Wales the catching of black bream has become in the last ten years a specialised art. Good places are where there is a rocky bottom with plenty of weed among which bream love to forage. Such spots are fairly common from Portland Bill right down to Land's End. It is a great pity that thousands of young bream are caught each year off the Cornish coast and used as bait for other fish. In their immature state in this part of the country they are called chad.

Both species can be taken on a drifting line or by paternoster, but my best sport has always been when using a ledger. There is no need to use heavy tackle because it is only on rare occasions that four or five pounders are taken. A sea trout fly rod is an excellent tool although on many occasions when fishing the Menai Straits (Wales) I have had quite a lot of fun with an old greenheart trout rod.

Once a shoal of good fish has been located they can be kept around for quite a time by the frequent use of ground bait. The usual ingredients are chopped lugworms and crushed mussels and crabs. A favourite bait is lugworm and a good type of hook is a No. 10 Model Perfect long shank.

Cod fishing to be really good should be practised from late autumn until early spring. Cod are rarely caught in shallow water, preferring the deeps where it prowls near the bottom and feeds on seaworms and various shell-fish.

However, during late autumn and winter some excellent bags are made by long casting from beaches that shelve sharply to very deep water and from rocks near tidal pools. One can ledger for them or use paternosters holding two or three booms and hooks. Long shanked hooks are best as cod usually get the hook well down and a log shank is more easy to disgorge.

While it is by no means a fish to be classed in the sporting category its qualities as a food fish are unrivalled. Baits include lugworm, mussel, crab and fish flesh. My best takes have always been when fishing off the west coast of Scotland, the area around Cape Wrath being exceedingly good.

Haddock are also plentiful off the west coast of Scotland, but not much in evidence in the south. Methods in angling for them are similar to those employed for cod. From March to October is usually the best period of the year to fish for this valuable food fish. Suitable hooks are No. 2 or 3 long shank.

Hake is not a fish much sought after by the amateur angler. Method of fishing, baits and hooks are the same as for cod.

Whiting inhabit fairly shallow water and 20 to 30 fathoms are usual depths at which they are found. To get the best sport out of whiting, light tackle is advisable as the average weight is from a pound to three pounds. A four pounder ranks as a specimen. The largest fish during the last few years have been taken from the little fishing station of Shieldaig (Scotland), the nearest railway station being Strathcarron. At Shieldaig I have enjoyed myself on more than one occasion.

This fish likes sandy ground and during the summer months feeds fairly close inshore. A three boom paternoster is the ideal tackle and it is not an uncommon occurrence to take three at a time once the right depth has been ascertained. No. 5 or 6 hooks are good and should be baited with lugworm, mussel, herring or mackerel flesh.

Pouting can be taken on the same tackle as whiting, but the hooks should be two sizes smaller. This species love rocks and any station where there are sunken reefs is well worth a trial for this fish the average weight of which is about three-quarters of a pound. A two-pounder is considered a specimen.

Turbot are more plentiful these days than they have been for at least 25 years. If fishing a mark known to hold this fish strong tackle is advisable. The only two I ever caught were taken on a handline off Margate with a live sand-eel as bait. The most common size of this fish is from four to ten pounds.

Ling are not much sought after by the amateur, but when after cod or haddock it is quite possible that one will be caught. Tackle, baits and hooks the same as cod.

John Dory are usually taken when fishing for other species near the sea bed. It is rarely caught on the east coast but is fairly common off Devon and Cornwall. Its average weight is from four to five pounds. On one occasion while bass fishing at Mevagissey my son landed a small one of three pounds on a live prawn that is the only one I have seen caught. In Mounts Bay they are fairly common. They are delicious eating and taste not unlike a plaice.

Wrasse are among the most brilliant coloured fish that inhabit our waters. They put up a fair fight on light tackle. There are seven species and all are characterised by their thick lips. They inhabit rocky areas and are often taken when after coalfish or pollack. The two most common are the ballan and cuckoo. They are mostly caught along the south and west coasts.

Tope are sporting fish and fairly common around our coasts with the largest frequenting the Kent coastline. They are often taken when pollack fishing but the best tackle is that used for conger fishing. Mackerel, herring, pilchard and squid are excellent baits. Fighting hard when hooked it is not uncommon for the angler to lose line and tackle in the first run after the hook has been set.

It has a very tough-skinned mouth and the strike should be hard, but delayed until the fish has moved off 15 or 20 yards with the bait, otherwise it will be pulled out of the tope's mouth without the hooks engaging.

A motor boat is advisable and the stations from which tope anglers embark are usually well supplied with boats, tackle and baits.

MAKE A NOTE OF THESE

Good stations for boat fishing include the following: NORTHUMBERLAND: Alnmouth, Craster, Whitley Bay. *Fish* one can expect include pollack, whiting, codling, gurnard, flounder, plaice and coalfish.

YORKSHIRE: Bridlington, Filey, Whitby, Scarborough and Flamborough. *Fish:* Codling, flatfish, whiting, mackerel during the summer, gurnard, pollack and coalfish.

NORFOLK: Yarmouth, Cromer, Palling-on-Sea. *Fish:* Flatfish, mackerel, whiting and occasional bass.

SUFFOLK: Lowestoft, Felixstowe. *Fish:* Bass, skate, flatfish, codling and mullet.

ESSEX: Clacton, Southend-on-Sea. *Fish:* Flatfish, skate, codling, pouting and whiting.

KENT: Herne Bay, Broadstairs, Margate, Dover, Deal, Dungeness, Sandgate and Hythe. *Fish:* Conger, tope, bass, pouting, mackerel, whiting and most flatfish.

SUSSEX: Hastings, Bexhill, Brighton, Littlehampton, New-haven, Seaford and Hove. *Fish:* Bass, conger, cod, whiting, mackerel, bream, gurnard, ling and most species of flatfish.

HANTS.: Bournemouth and Southsea. *Fish:* Bass, mullet, conger, skate and mackerel.

DORSET: Bridport, Poole, Swanage. *Fish:* Bass, mullet, bream, skate, wrasse, pollack, whiting and mackerel.

DEVON: Torquay, Dartmouth, Plymouth, Dawlish, Seaton, Ilfracombe and Salcombe. *Fish:* Bass, coalfish, gurnard, pollack, whiting, bream, mackerel, conger, pouting, most flat-fish and occasional mullet.

CORNWALL: Polperro, Penzance, Mousehole, Porthleven, Looe, Mevagissey, Newquay and Fowey. *Fish:* Bass, pollack, conger, skate, bream, ling, tope, whiting and mackerel. From most of the Cornish stations there is always the chance of the angler hooking a John Dory.

WALES (PEMBROKE): Tenby. *Fish:* Pollack, whiting, mackerel and on occasions flatfish.

CARNARVON: Penmaenmawr and Llandudno. *Fish:* Pollack, bass, mackerel, whiting, conger, coalfish, codling and flatfish.

ISLE OF MAN: Port St. Mary, Port Erin, Peel and Ramsey are among the best stations on the island. *Fish:* Ling, conger, haddock, mackerel, pollack, skate, wrasse, bass and flatfish.

SCOTLAND: There are many fine stations on the west coast, but transport is not of the best. The places visited by the author include, Cape Wrath, Sheigra, Loch Inver (Sutherland); Gairloch, Loch Torridon and Shieldaig (Ross and Cromarty).

IRELAND: The best stations for a visitor are without a doubt Achill, Ballycotton, Valentia, Kilmore Quay, Youghal, Glengarriff and Ardmore. When visiting any of these places it is best to book your boat well in advance as during the height of the holiday season there is a great demand. The Irish Tourist Association of 14, Upper O'Connell Street, Dublin will supply all information required, free.

ISLE OF WIGHT: Ryde, Shanklin, Sandown and Osborne. *Fish:* Bass, mackerel, conger, pouting, tope, whiting, flatfish and occasional black bream.

SALMON AND SEA TROUT

I have left these two species till last for the simple reason that while thousands are taken every year by the angler fishing freshwater, quite a large number are caught in salt-water. England, Wales and Ireland offers very few places where this type of sport can be engaged in, but in Scotland there are numerous sea lochs in which the boat angler can thoroughly enjoy himself.

On the west coast of Scotland from Cape Wrath down to Loch Fyne there are many spots where fly fishing can be just as profitable as fishing the best of rivers.

If the fish are not interested in flies the spinning rod can be used with small spoons or devons as bait. Or one can troll a sprat, minnow or prawn with a fair chance of success during mid-season when the fish are congregated in the loch waiting for a flood to assist them to get up the rivers and streams which flow into it.

Frankly the first two methods are best, providing one has a good boatman who is aware where the fish lie, therefore it is always a good policy to engage a boatman who is himself an angler.

It was in 1932 that I had my first taste of salt-water fishing for salmon and sea trout, and until then had never really understood what these fish were really capable of in the way of fighting for their freedom. Perfection! It is a strong word. Yet what other can be used which will not appear feeble when applied to them.

A friend had secured permission for me to have the use of a boat on a sea loch. At first it was a question of trial and error on the question of baits, but after a couple of days I found that during early morning and throughout brilliant sun-shine my best sport with salmon was when using a prawn on the spinning rod. In the evening the sea trout came on to the fly. During that memorable week my take was nine salmon and 25 sea trout.

Now let us look at the question a little closer, because in salt-water fishing for these two species a little different technique has to be applied. There are quite a few salmon and sea trout anglers who claim that flies, devons, spoons and sprats will solve just about any problem which has to do with rods and these gamesters. Such assertions usually come from people whose experience is limited to purely local conditions. Often they fish when their favourite baits are most effective. And not infrequently they are deaf to the advantages to be had from using other methods.

Many an angler has become wedded to a particular set of tactics and a particular sort of bait because he has had an exceptional run of luck with it. However, to use such experience as a basis for concentrating on the one method and bait no matter where the fishing is done is foolish. It will not bring the best results when considered from the season-round point of view.

During a dry season when the fish have been waiting in the lochs for a flood so that they can ascend the rivers for spawning, a prawn is one of the best baits I have tried and the brighter the sun the better it takes. A salmon usually takes a fly in a languorous sophisticated sort of way, like a well-fed human picking out a tit-bit. But just work a prawn in the area where he exercises himself by going for short swims from his lie. He'll make the water fly in a frenzied effort to grab it before it gets away. This no doubt is because he is more or less a sea fish and still likes sea food, but why a pink prawn should attract him I have never been able to understand beyond the fact that while in sea water he may still to a large extent feed by smell, therefore, although the bait is pink it would still have the smell that the fish associated with a succulent bit of food.

LOSES MORE FISH

While the prawn under certain conditions is a deadly bait it has been my experience that it probably hooks more strikes, but loses more hooked fish than any other method. This no doubt is due to the fact that a salmon hooked on prawn in salt-water acts a little differently to one hooked on the same kind of bait in a river. As soon as he feels the hooks he shakes his head violently and leaps all over the place. I appreciate to the full that it is dangerous to make such a sweeping statement, but out of 18 salmon taken by me in sea water not one altered his tactics. The hooks with which the prawn is armed are on the small side and the hold being shallow often works loose under such treatment.

Lochs in which there are an abundance of large underwater rocks and shelves provide excellent places for the prawn. One can spin it or work it without a spinner attachment in much the same way as a salmon fly, using the fly rod to cast it. The trace should never be less than 10-lb. breaking strain, it can be wire or nylon, but if spinning it is always advisable to use an anti-kink on the trace if the line is braided nylon. With nylon monofilm it is not necessary, but a small half-moon lead nipped on to the trace will ensure the bait sinking a few feet.

Most prawn tackles on the market have treble hooks, but for use with a fly rod double hooks are best, one at the head and another in the middle of the body. A tackle I can recommend is "The Test". The needle of the tackle is pushed through the centre of the prawn and the hooks are bound in position with pink sewing cotton.

I have never had much sport with large prawns, the best size in my opinion is what is known as medium, about 2½ inches long.

To be on the safe side it is always best to have a jar of preserved prawns in the tackle bag just in case there is no shop handy from which to purchase a supply. As I write this there stands on my desk a couple of jars of salted prawns that I have just screwed down. Such baits will last a long time if screw-type lid jars are used. A pint of prawns will cost quite a lot, but will provide enough medium-sized ones for two jars of about 12 in each. Put a layer of salt in the bottom of the jar, next put in your prawns head downwards and when the jar is full fill the remaining space with salt, the coarser the salt is the better. Put the lid on tight and give the jar a good shaking so that the baits are covered with salt.

They can also be preserved in strong brine and also glycerine. In the former a two inch layer of salt is placed in the bottom of the jar, the prawns are placed as before, head downwards, more salt is put on top and the jar is then filled with water to absorb the salt. In glycerine they will last for months, but my luck has been out when using prawns so preserved. No matter which method you use be sure that the jar is completely air-tight when the lid is screwed down or your time and trouble will have been wasted.

SOME GOOD FLIES

Flies for sea lochs when salmon are being sought include such favourites as Thunder and Lightning, Jack Scott, Black Doctor, Silver Wilkinson, Durham Ranger, Black Goshawk, Golden Olive, Blue Charm and Silver Doctor.

In artificial metal baits a two inch blue and silver devon is always worth a try and so is a gold and silver $1\frac{1}{2}$ inch spoon.

Small shrimps are good for sea trout worked in the same way as salmon but invariably it will be found that the most consistant sport will be had on flies, the cast containing two which should be sunk well down.

Here is a good collection: Teal and Black, Teal and Red, Teal and Claret, Peter Ross, Butcher, Alexandra, Silver March Brown, Red Spinner, Golden Olive, Fiery Brown, Zulu (Red) and Woodcock and Red.

One last word, for the novice there is no better way of

starting to fish for salmon and sea trout than in a sea loch.*
There are no obstacles to steer the fish away from and providing
one keeps cool and the hook holds there is no reason why the
fish should not be boated, after all you have the whole loch to
play him in. And what play!

*Readers are referred to the same author's *Technique of Freshwater Fishing*, see notice at the end of this book.

CHAPTER VII

SPINNING

Thread-line fishing or spinning as it is more commonly called will always afford the maximum in sport and because it is a little unusual it appeals to the normal angler. For centuries, fishermen have been on the lookout for new methods. At first the spinning reel was used exclusively by freshwater anglers and it was not until a few years ago that the sea angler realised that such a reel overcame many difficulties. For my part there is something about a threadline reel that tickles the imagination. The ease with which the lightest bait can be sent in its search for fish has never ceased to fascinate me.

Spinning is mainly a summer and autumn pastime for then the enthusiast's fish such as mackerel, bass, pollack and coalfish are working near the surface and lightweight lines can be used. As the water cools with the advance of winter the fish go deeper and heavier lines are needed to offset the weight needed to carry the bait down.

Lines of light weight five to eight pound breaking strain will cast much further than heavy diameter ten and fifteen pound test lines, but light lines wear out faster and often as not break in a snag or large fish. You've got to make a compromise somewhere. Check the last few feet of your line for weak spots after a day's fishing as this is the area that takes the jolts from casting, snagging and immersion.

With a light weight line one can use a very light rod and still take heavy fish, but with a heavy line the rod has to be strong also to counter-balance the weight of the line.

While the usual spinning baits are devons, wagtails, prawns, spoons and natural baits to which spinners have been fixed the author has had quite good sport with mackerel and pollack when using a weighted artificial fly. A couple of split shot nipped on to the trace near the eye of the fly is all that is required to ensure it will get well below the surface and while the angler using a paternoster or ledger is waiting for fish to move into the vicinity of his offering the spinning enthusiast can be sending his bait out to find the fish wherever they may be. The amount of water that can be covered by spinning is greater than by any of the other fishing means. The trolling fisherman though he moves his bait, covers far less water than the spinner.

Many sea anglers have a notion that spinning is a waste of time, but their trouble is that they have condemned the method before they have even tried it. The basic principles of salt-water spinning are the same as those which govern freshwater. Do not move the bait through the water as though you were afraid that the fish would bite; give them plenty of time. More fish are lost because the bait is moving too rapidly than are gained.

LET THE BAIT SINK

For pollack, coalfish and bass let the bait sink well down before making the retrieve and then work it in a sink and draw motion. In other words give the reel handle a few quick turns then stop for a second and repeat. When you stop turning the handle the bait will drop downwards in a series of gyrating tumbling motions. For mackerel, particularly in July and August a bait worked near the surface will provide quite a lot of fun. Mackerel more so than most fish are curious regarding moving objects which happen to pass within range of their vision.

The idea in using artificial baits is to represent the living fish or worm, therefore a little care in preparing the tackle is always worth while. The trace is equipped with swivels at either end and an anti-kink to prevent the line from twisting.

The anti-kick can be of celluloid if fishing near the surface and of lead if depth is required.

With the threadline I have found that the only safe way to handle large fish after they have made their first run is by pumping. If you reel against the weight of the fish, each turn of the handle lays a twist in the line. To pump merely bring your rod tip from horizontal to vertical bending the rod against the fish. This can be done without endangering the rod if you do it slowly. When the rod is at vertical quickly lower it to horizontal, reeling at the same time. In effect you are gaining a few feet at a time, but it is the steady pressure that wears a fish down. Once he tires his fins stop working and he is thrown off "balance". You can then ease him to the surface and the gaff or net will do the rest.

There are places round our coasts sheltering pollack, coal-fish and bass just waiting for the man with the spinner, but he must know his job. It is no use just casting a bait anywhere and hoping for the best. An old Scottish boatman once said to me, "If you want to catch fish you have to think like a fish".

One of the first spinning reels I had was a Malloch, but for the last fifteen years my favourite has been the Altex. It is well-nigh foolproof and will stand up to any amount of hard work. I also use an Ambassadeur 6000.

The secret of good spinning is to take your time. Every inch of water within reach should be fished carefully, parti-cularly where the sea bed is rocky for it is in such localities that pollack love to roam. And the best time to spin for them is when the tide is in for then they come out of their hides to scour the rocks for food.

BEST ALL-ROUND BAIT

I have often been asked what in my opinion is the best all-round spinning bait and each time have answered "the spoon". This spinning, wobbling artificial is the most ancient of devices for luring fish and it is a great pity that its capabilities as a creel-filler are possibly the most underrated of any bait in the tackle box.

It is thirty years since I realised the possibilities of fishing a spoon. Until then, my pollack, coalfish and mackerel had been taken on flies and devons. Then my work entailed a visit to China, where I found the natives using kidney-shaped spoons made of mother-of-pearl. On inquiry I found that such spoons were in use long before bone hooks dressed with dyed fibres and silk had been thought of. Some years later in British Columbia I found the Indians taking sea fish with bone spoons; and was told that the method of making and fishing these spoons had been handed down from father to son for generations. In Finland and Norway, the story was the same. Spoons had been the ancient's fish-getter.

I am convinced that fewer strikes are obtained on a dull than a bright spoon. It is the flash of the artificial which attracts. Spoons should, therefore, be kept well polished. Copper, brass (gold) and silver spoons are specifically chosen because they resemble more or less the fry upon which predatory fish feed. On very bright days and during the neap tides a copper spoon is preferred. Silver or gold give better results on cloudy or dull days. Chromium, incidentally, has the appearance of nickel when out of water; but in water it takes on a dark hue and for this reason is rarely used.

SOUND FISHING

When using large spoons, or for that matter any heavy artificial bait, do not snatch them from the water; this puts a heavy strain on the tip of the rod. Bring the bait to the surface and pick it up quietly. This is moreover, sound fishing, for on many occasions a fish will follow the spoon up and take it as it reaches the surface.

Next to the spoon I place the rubber eel second for obtaining sport. In 1951 the rubber eel proved its worth when my boat companion the late Mr. Copping landed a 16-lb. coalfish on an outsize in eels, a 15 inch one. "Old Cop" as he was called by sea anglers over a wide area believed in the old principle of "big fish, big baits". One thing about his rubber eels I noticed which may have accounted for his having more strikes than me, was that at the tail of his bait

"COPPINGS" RUBBER EEL

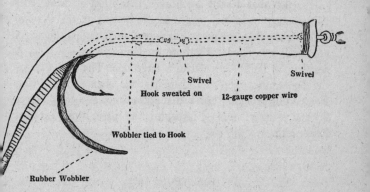

Swivel

Swivel

Hook sweated on

12-gauge copper wire

Wobbler tied to Hook

Rubber Wobbler

he had fastened a wobbler. This wobbler was made out of a rubber washer used for sealing preserve jars. The washer is cut in half and a half is fastened to the hook inside the rubber. As the eel spins through the water the wobbler creates a "boiling" in the water and this so far as coalfish are concerned, proves attractive.

"Old Cop" had his own method of making rubber eels and having tried them on several occasions I can vouch for their effectiveness. Inside the rubber tubing he put a length of 12 gauge soft copper wire. The ends are sweated to swivels and the hook is sweated to the tailend swivel. The beauty of this eel is that as soon as you have a strike the eel straightens out and you then have a direct pull on the fish. When you have landed or lost your fish as the case might be it is an easy matter to bend the bait into any curve to make it spin either left or right.

In third place come devons and wagtails. With these two baits you never know what you might catch. For instance a friend of mine some years ago was spinning a three inch gold devon for coalfish on Loch Torridon and the first strike he got was from a 15-lb salmon which was duly landed after a battle lasting ten minutes.

The fact that devons are heavier than most artificial baits is most helpful as less weight has to be put on the trace to get distance. Another point I like about them is that the hooks are small compared with those used on spoons and eels. A small hook holds better than a large one. The fine wire of the hook bites deep and there is little chance of it being levered out providing the fish is played nice and easy. Never try and bring a fish in by force, it is the surest way I know of losing him.

FOR SCHOOL BASS

Wagtails are good for school bass and also mackerel when the fish are near the surface and so one or two coloured red and blue should always be included in the tackle box.

During those periods when fish evince little desire to have a go spinning baits can be made more attractive by attaching a small mackerel lask on the hook. The skin from the tail end of a freshly caught herring or pilchard is also good if used as a lask on a spinning bait. On occasions a herring lask can be more deadly than mackerel due no doubt to the fact that some herrings have more oil in their skins than others and as the bait is drawn through the water there is an oily smell which fish follow.

So far we have discussed artificial spinning baits, what about the natural ones? The only ones I have ever had any luck with are sand-eels, prawn and shrimp.

Some anglers prefer to thread their tackle through the middle of an eel and then fix the spinner on, but the writer has found that by cutting off the head of the eel and putting the needle of the tackle through the body of the eel and tying the hooks into position with fine fuse wire is simpler and better.

Never be surprised at anything you may get when using this bait. Salmon, sea trout, coalfish, pollack and bass have all fallen for it, and will continue to do so for the simple reason that where there is plenty of sand this eel forms the staple diet of many fish.

Prawns and also shrimps are good summer spinning baits and an ideal time to use these naturals are when fish are feeding near the surface as indicated by the gulls which congregate overhead. Tackle for prawn and shrimp fishing has already been dealt with in Chapter III.

Many anglers use wire traces and after much use the wire sometimes acquires curves and kinks that handicap the functioning of the swivels. These curves, once acquired, are difficult to remove either by stretching or stroking.

Try this method if you are without another trace. Fasten one end of the trace to a nail. Hold the other end by the fingers of one hand. Now light a wooden match and move the flame back and forth along the trace's length while it is held tightly. This trick will often straighten out some pretty bad kinks.

Finally, carry a bit of chamois leather at all times in a pocket of your fishing coat. The material will prove invaluable for rubbing the line down occasionally during the day. This is a good habit to get into, for it adds to the life of the line, besides keeping it free of grit and hence usable for longer periods.

PURCHASING A ROD

When you buy a spinning rod, be sure to examine the rings – you might examine the rings of some that you now have – to see if there's varnish on them; there very often is, even on good rods.

This varnish can become very hard, and through wear it will develop hard edges, to scrape and cut the line passing through. This, naturally, greatly reduces the life of a line – complaints of a line breaking when a big fish has been hooked is due, nine times out of ten, to varnish on the rod rings having weakened the line.

The cure is very simple. Merely scrape that varnish off carefully.

A NEW FIELD

To sum up. For these fishermen who enjoy taking pot luck off the rocks, casting for whatever may come along, spinning equipment offers an entirely new field of angling. However, if you are a fisherman who wants to forego the fun of playing a fish in order to quickly drag him in and cast for another, the spinning method is not for you. If, however, your sporting instincts are sufficiently aroused to enjoy trying to land a good fish on light tackle you will find in spinning a fascinating way to pursue the art of angling.

I think that spinning – real spinning – goes far beyond all other methods of sea angling in intricacy of design and complexity of pattern. Its mastery passes beyond things teachable and understandable, into a region of instinct, feeling or sixth sense.

The angler who spins for his fish must project part of his brains and nerves through the rod, down the line and into the bait to make that bait act in a manner acceptable to good fish. I'm speaking, of course, of the rule, not the exception. Master anglers have some unnamed sense which enable them, unconsciously perhaps, to assemble and evaluate the conditions of the varying moods of the sea and deduce the proper thing to do, but if their lives depended on it they could not tell how they came by it. It's experience and experience can only be gained by practice and the best place to put in that practice is of course – on the sea.

CHAPTER VIII

WINTER FISHING

When November comes round many anglers put their tackle away till the following spring and in so doing miss some good sport. Mark you it is cold work and one has to be dressed warmly to stand up to it.

One of the principal winter fish is the cod. During the warm months this species keeps to the very deep water but as soon as the colder weather sets in they move into the near coastal waters.

Codfish cannot be considered game fish but what they lack in gameness is more than balanced by their value as food. When close inshore they eat worms, shrimps, prawns and sand-eels and the angler who has taken the precaution of preserving some of these baits in the summer need not worry.

The hooks on the paternoster should be larger for winter fishing to hold big baits. When using prawn my method is to put on a couple of big ones and if using fish flesh such as herring or mackerel a large piece will be found to attract the really large cod more than little baits.

Quiet rocky bays are good spots providing there is about 20 or more fathoms of water at high tide.

Another fish which provides sport to the winter angler is the pollack. These marauders from the ocean invade the rock-bound coves and bays and usually bite better in the colder months than in the summer, but whereas in the summer they were found near the surface the angler will find his best sport will be had when his baits are well down.

Once a pollack has been caught there is no need for the angler to move because where there is one there will be more as they move around in schools.

The printed page in my typewriter fades before my eyes and Land's End comes into focus for it was in a little bay there that I had some really wonderful sport among the pollack during a couple of days in the month of December.

Each fish I took was lured by a preserved sand-eel and the thing that struck me most about winter pollacking was that the fish fought like tigers.

Another point was that the fish I caught were taken on the incoming tide. The line should be nothing less than 10-lb. breaking strain; when the hook goes home a pollack immediately makes for the rocks and a little pressure is needed to keep him moving. Should he reach his objective the chances are he will snag the tackle round the rocks and your hope of slipping the net under him is about nil.

When the wind is light or blowing off-shore and when the water is calm is good pollack weather no matter how cold it might be.

APPETITES ARE SHARPENED

The whiting is another cold weather fish which can be taken close inshore providing the sea bed is sand and once a shoal has been located the angler is in for quite a bit of fun for the cold seems to sharpen their appetites. It is not an uncommon occurrence to hook two and sometimes three at once. In December I have found them particularly partial to salted shrimps and small prawns fished either with a ledger or three-hook paternoster.

The haddock is another fish that is worth going after, but the best chances of capturing one or two is by using a boat. The haddock is a great wanderer in its search for food and as a result the angler *must* know the sea-bed he is fishing over. It prefers pebbly and sandy bottoms during winter. Once you have discovered such a place in an area frequented by this species you will not have to wait long before the haddock will be there turning over the pebbles with their snouts in search of sustenance.

In trolling from a boat at this period of the year it is advisable to use heavier leads than those used in summer. You have to get the baits down and with currents much stronger you want to be sure that your offering is down where the fish are. For such work a light rod is not advisable and for this reason my winter rod for boat work is fairly stiff to withstand the extra strain of towing a good length of line and heavy weight.

Before setting out for a day's winter fishing, particularly from a boat it is always advisable to have a look at the barometer. The changes that take place in the atmosphere are principally marked by the rising and falling of the barometer and one of the worst days for boat fishing is when there is a strong wind blowing for under these conditions it is impossible to keep your bait in position.

The rise and fall indicated on the dial of a barometer is apparently caused by heat and cold. By the former the atmosphere is lightened and by the latter it is condensed and becomes heavy.

The barometer falls suddenly while the air is expanded before a gale of wind and rises again gradually as the condensed air returns, and the wind in like manner subsides.

In winter a rising barometer foretells frost and in frosty weather if the mercury falls three or four divisions a thaw is on its way, but in a continued frost if the glass rises it will certainly snow.

When a storm happens soon after the falling of the glass expect but little of it and likewise expect but little fair weather when it proves fair shortly after the mercury has risen. The barometer is always highest during a long frost and the rising usually takes place with a north-east wind. With a south-west wind the barometer drops.

OF SHORT DURATION

When the barometer is low for the season there is seldom a great weight of rain, though a fair day in such a case is rare. The general tenor of the weather at such times is short with sudden showers and squalls of wind from the south-west or north-west.

When the appearances of the sky are very promising for fair and the barometer at the same time low it may be depended upon that the appearance will not continue so long, always remember that during the winter months the sky changes very suddenly. One minute the sky is high and clear and the next sees dense clouds rolling in from the horizon.

Many seasoned sea anglers are able up to a point to forecast the weather, but for my part I shall always pin my faith in the barometer and when it rises or is stationary for any length of time then I fish. On the other hand when it falls rapidly or the needle varies more than three points in a few hours I leave the tackle in the bag and content myself with the thought that the sooner the storm breaks the sooner it will be over.

In boat fishing it never pays to take chances with the weather at this time of the year, therefore anything that will assist the angler to tell in advance what weather to expect is to say the least more than helpful. For my part I feel fairly confident that if the barometer was understood more by anglers there would be fewer boating fatalities.

One last word. Winter fishing is both hard on the tackle and the angler. Wrap up as warm as you can with an extra pair of socks in the bag in case of wet feet, not forgetting an oil-skin coat in case of storms.

CHAPTER IX

IDENTIFYING THE CATCH

GENERAL FEATURES OF SEA FISH

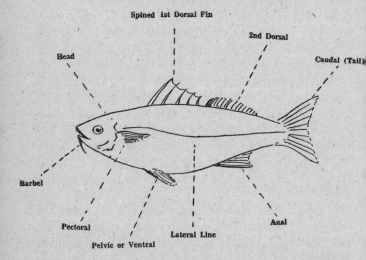

Headed by the acrobatic, breath-taking tunny, the lightning-fast bass, the graceful mullet and slashing mackerel, more than 200 varieties of fish visit the waters washing our coasts. The fun of fishing is greatly enhanced if the angler can identify his catch. In many species colour taken in conjunction with other features can be a good guide, but colour by itself is never really reliable as there are so many variations.

Fins and shape of body are also good clues. For instance no one seeing a John Dory would ever mistake the fish again.

The pollack and coalfish are practically similar to the uninitiated, but there is a great difference if you know what to look for, the pollack has a protruding bottom jaw.

Excluding flat fish the majority of the other species have fins disposed in two sets. One set includes those fins which exist in the middle line of the fish and which are therefore single or unpaired. Such as the back fins, the tail fin and the anal fin or that on the lower surface or lower margin of the body. Then there are those fins which always exist in pairs – one on each side – and which in reality represent the paired limbs of higher animals. These paired fins never exceed two pairs in number. The two fins at the breast are called pectoral. The other and remaining pair are named ventral or pelvic fins. In such fish as the cod, the ventral fins are situated on the throat beneath the pectorals.

The soles, flounders, and their allies, as every one knows, possess bodies which are literally fringed by long fins of varying breadth. Furthermore on either broad surface of the fish we see a single and prominent fin, and also two fins below; one existing on each side of the fish. With what fins in ordinary fishes do the fins of the flat-fishes correspond? The question is readily answered by a reference to what we have ascertained regarding the belongings of our common fishes. The long fin which fringes what we may call the upper edge of the body in the flat-fish, and which thus exists in the middle line of the body, must be the back fin. Similarly the fin which borders the lower edge of the body must represent a long anal fin; this fin being very short as a rule in other fishes. The single fin on each broad surface of the flat-fish must be a breast fin and the two fins below are the ventral fins.

Almost all fishes are compressed from side to side. That is, the sides form the most prominent surfaces in a fish. The back and belly of an ordinary fish are mere lines as it were and correspond somewhat to the mathematical definition of a line in that they represent length without breadth.

This chapter has been included for one purpose, to afford a little guidance in identifying the catch. It is not proposed to deal with every fish, that would take volumes, rather it is to catalogue those that are likely to be met with when out for a day's fishing. The sketches are from fish taken by the author, his son and friends and from specimens in various museums.

BASS

One of the first fish I ever caught in the sea was a bass at Aberdovey (Wales) and with its capture there was presented a problem. What was it? A fish of 2½ lbs., it had the appearance of a sea trout even to a number of dark spots on its sides. However, my father soon enlightened me. The bass is a sea perch and like its freshwater relative it has two dorsal fins, the first nearest the head, has nine spikes. The predominant colour is silver with the back a bluish silver with a dark spot on the gill-cover. In its youthful stage it is known as a school bass and at this stage is called, in many places on the south

BASS

coast, salmon bass or white salmon. The pectoral fins in adult specimens are tinged with pink while the other fins are silvery grey. In taking a large bass off the hook care should be exercised as the gill-covers have numerous spikes on them. The dorsal spines can also inflict a nasty wound. It is an excellent food fish.

BREAMS

There are several sea breams, but only two will be dealt with here, the common or red bream and the black bream. The former is a most brilliantly coloured fish being red

RED BREAM

BLACK BREAM

suffused with gold. It has a long spiny dorsal fin and when full grown has a large dark spot on the shoulder. When young they are called chads and are often used for bait by professional fishermen in Cornwall. As a food fish it is excellent.

The black bream is not so common as the red and in my opinion is not such a good food fish. In colour it is a dark bluish grey merging into nearly black on the back with four or five pale golden horizontal lines below the lateral line which is very clearly defined.

Both breams are summer visitors, the black providing the better sport as it is much the stronger fighter.

COD

The cod is one of the most predacious of fish; it loves deep and cold water. It has a well defined barbel on chin

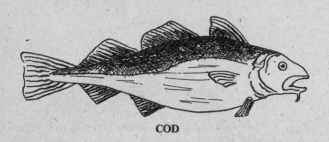

COD

and a well-marked lateral line of a dirty white colour. The general colour is olive green merging below the lateral line into a greenish yellow and then into dirty white on the belly. There are numerous dark spots and markings resembling grey marble. It has three dorsal fins and two anal, all of which are soft and minus spines. The young cod frequently come close inshore and are known as codling. As a food fish it is one of the best.

CONGER EEL

This sea eel is easily recognised from its fresh-water brother, firstly it is scaleless, secondly the eyes are very large and in the larger specimens often protruding, and thirdly the gills are very large. In addition the teeth are powerful. The

CONGER EEL

reason I make this comparison is because quite a number of fresh-water eels are taken in salt-water every year. The conger is a fine food fish and well worth all the trouble it takes to catch him.

DAB

This flat-fish frequents the whole of our coastline and is often met in the estuaries late in the season. It is among the smallest of flat-fish, the record being a 2-lb. 9½-ozs. It can be easily recognised by a very distinct curve in the lateral line near the head and when full grown, particularly in the male,

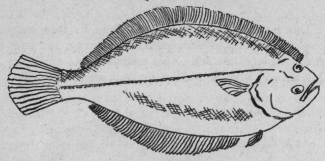

DAB

has a number of dark coloured spots on its back. It is quite good eating if cooked within a few hours of catching.

DORY (JOHN)

I have often heard the dory referred to as a hideous looking fish, but to me the dory looks like the Solomon of his tribe.

JOHN DORY

His expression denotes a melancholy resignation to the decrees of fate. His countenance is as impassively suggestive as a pantomime mask. But to take the dory on his own level, he is admitted by the most inspired authorities to possess an exquisite flavour and to furnish a meat of rare delicacy. Upon the whole, and admitting his scant claims to beauty, the dory is certainly a very interesting fellow. He rouses the antiquary, and puzzles the naturalist. He often goes by the name of St. Peter's fish. This no doubt is due to the large dark blotch on its sides, put there, says the legend, by the Apostle's fingers. The prevailing colour is brown, tinged with golden yellow. The spines of the large dorsal fin are sharp to the touch, and can inflict a nasty wound if handled carelessly.

FLOUNDER

Like the dab this member of the flat-fish tribe can be found all round our coasts and most of the estuaries. The lateral line is sharply defined with a slight curve over the pectoral fins. There are a number of tubercles along the base of the long

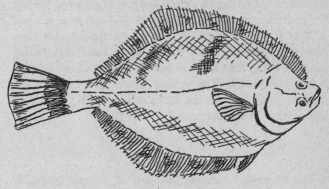

FLOUNDER

dorsal fin with smaller ones along the lateral line. The back, or upper surface, is in many specimens a very dark brown and in others black. The underside is a creamy white. It is nice eating when cooked within a couple of hours of catching.

HADDOCK

HADDOCK

With this fish legend has also been busy, again no doubt due to the large dark blotch above the pectoral fins put there, the legend says, by Christ's thumb and forefinger when feeding the multitude on loaves and fishes. Be that as it may, it is one of the most valuable of fish and a large industry has been built around it. The lateral line is dark coloured and the top jaw protrudes a little over the bottom. Barbel is small and just below bottom lip. The general colour is greyish brown merging into white for the flanks and abdomen. The tail is more forked than that of a cod.

HAKE

This is another valuable food fish of the cod family. It loves deep water and in shape is more slender and elongated than the cod. The lower jaw is slightly longer than the top and both are armed with very sharp teeth. The head is large

HAKE

and flat and looks out of place on so slender a fish. The fins are much larger than those of the cod, and the dorsals have soft spines.

HALIBUT

The largest of our flat-fish, the halibut is a lover of deep water. The lateral line curves above the pectoral fins and the jaws are powerful with the lower protruding. Both are armed

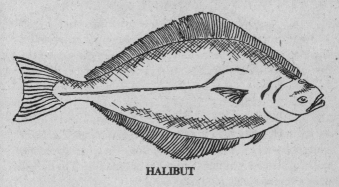

HALIBUT

with strong teeth. The upper surface is olive brown with the underside white. It is an excellent food fish.

LING

This member of the cod family has a long body and very narrow head with a barbel on the chin, the tail is rounded

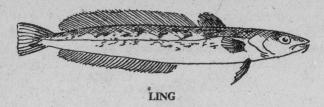

LING

and the fins are not so large as in the hake. It is olive brown in colour with numerous marbled markings on the back. It is a fairly good food fish.

MACKEREL

To my way of thinking, this is one of the most brightly coloured of our sea fish, the iridescence of the wavy bands

MACKEREL

on the back are beyond my powers of description. The lateral line comes well above the pectoral fins. There are two dorsal fins and six or seven finlets from the second dorsal to the tail. It is a very valuable food fish.

MULLETS

There are three grey mullets and although classed as sea fish they spend a good deal of their time in the estuaries, indeed most of the big ones caught have fallen to the angler fishing brackish water. The thick-lipped grey mullet is the most common. The colour of the back is greyish blue shading into silver on the flanks and belly. It has two very short dorsal fins and is minus a lateral line. There are numerous dark blue-grey lines or stripes on the flanks.

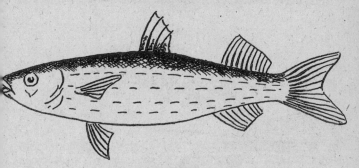

GREY MULLET

The thin-lipped variety is similar in appearance to the former, but has very thin lips instead of fleshy.

The golden grey mullet is a rare fish and is identified by two medium-sized golden spots on the gill covers.

The red mullet rarely frequents the estuaries, but is occasionally met with when fishing near rocks particularly off the Dorset coast. It is not such a shapely fish as the grey, but is much better from a culinary point of view. It is a reddish colour and has two barbels under the chin.

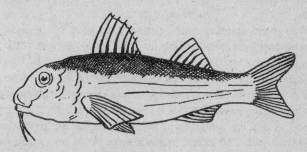

RED MULLET

PLAICE

Undoubtedly one of the sweetest eating of all flat-fish and it ranges all round our coasts. The lateral line has only a slight curve above the pectoral fins. The dorsal fin commences

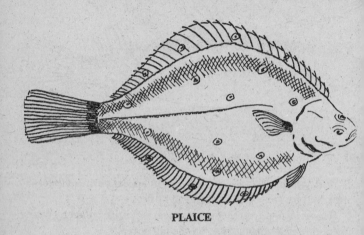

PLAICE

just behind the right eye and continues to within a short distance of the tail. The principal identifying feature is the numerous large red spots on the brown coloured back, fins and tail.

POLLACK AND COALFISH

A grand sporting fish but not such good eating as the other members of the cod family. It is a dark olive green colour on the back and has an underslung bottom jaw. The lateral line is strongly marked with a decided curve over the pectoral fins. Where there are rocks in plenty and an abundance of seaweed the largest pollack will be found.

The coalfish is similar in shape, but lacks the protruding bottom jaw. The lateral line is a dirty white colour and has only a slight curve over the pectoral fins. The colour is nearly

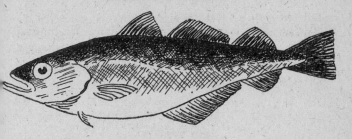

POLLACK

COALFISH

black with numerous marbled grey markings on the flanks.
There is also a small barbel below the chin.

POUT

This fish also a member of the cod tribe is commonly

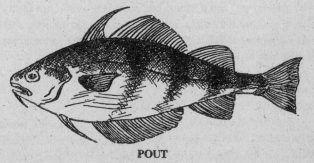

POUT

called bib. It is a squat-like shaped fish, being deep in the body, and is quite common around our eastern and southern coasts. Its colour is copper with four or five vertical bands of dark brown or black. It also has a barbel placed on the underside of the bottom lip. Its food value is not very great.

RED GURNARD

This fish is easily recognised by its colour which is a deep red and also by the spines on the pectoral fins. It is fairly common off the north-east coast.

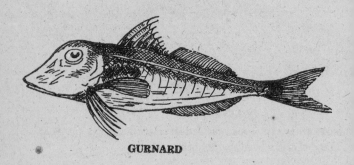

GURNARD

YELLOW GURNARD

Similar in shape to the red gurnard but the colour is more of an orange and the pectoral fins round the edges are steely blue in colour. It is often mistaken for the red variety, and is a nice flavoured fish. Great care should be taken in handling all gurnards as the spines are very sharp.

COMMON SKATE

A member of the ray family it is easily distinguished from other rays by the colouring of the underside which is a bluish white. It is this characteristic which has led to its being called

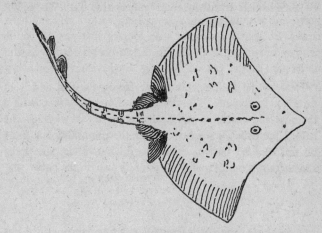

SKATE

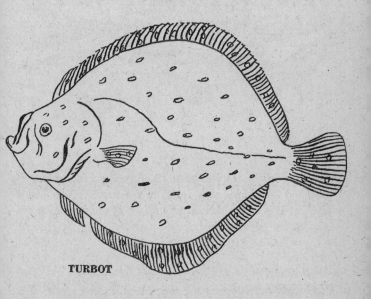

TURBOT

by some anglers grey skate and by others blue skate. The colour of the back is greyish brown.

TURBOT

Next to the halibut this is our largest flat-fish and is of excellent food value. The dorsal fin commences just behind the nose and continues practically to the tail fin muscle. The lateral line makes a semi-circle over the pectoral fins and the brown coloured back is covered with numerous dark spots and there is a number of bony pimples also on the back.

TOPE

A relative of the shark family it is a fine sporting fish, but of little or no use as food. As in all sharks its jaws are armed

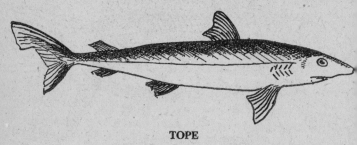

TOPE

with formidable serrated teeth. The predominant colour is grey and the skin is very rough to the touch, resembling a fine file. It is easily identified by reason of the tail which has a notch on the lower lobe.

WHITING

A small, but sweet-tasting member of the cod species it is easily recognised by the pearly white colour of its sides and

the absence of a barbel. It has a slim body and a fairly large
head for so small a fish.

WHITING

CUCKOO WRASSE

WRASSE

A beautiful coloured species, but useless for food. There
are seven varieties all of which have thick fleshy lips and
are brilliantly coloured. The two most common are the ballan
wrasse and the cuckoo wrasse. In all species the dorsal fin
is long, a third of it having spines. The predominant colours
in all the wrasses is blue, red, yellow and gold, these however
soon fade after death.

SALMON

When this grand fish reaches the adult stage it is an easy matter to identify it. The powerful tail fin has no fork in it but in the parr (young) stage it has and it is quite a difficult

SALMON

matter at times to tell a young salmon from an immature trout. Another feature of the salmon after it has been to the sea is that there are no black spots below the lateral line. The male salmon after they have been in fresh water develop a large hook to the lower jaw which is used in fighting off other male fish during the spawning period. The male salmon also turns a reddish tinge during autumn and it is then he is known as a "red fish". The sketch is of a male salmon of 18-lb. taken by the author's son from the Coquet (Northumberland) on a blue and silver devon one September.

SEA TROUT

As the salmon is known as the king of game fish, so is this member of the salmon family called, and rightly so, the prince. In build it is more streamlined than a salmon. There is always a fork in the tail and the spots reach below the

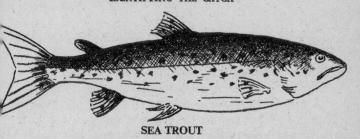

SEA TROUT

ventral fin and the gill covers are slightly more rounded. It has many names, for instance it is known as a white trout in Ireland, a peal in Devonshire, in Scotland whitling and herling when two pound or under in weight and sewin in many parts of Wales. To eat, oh boy!

CURIOUS FISH

Anything can happen when one is fishing from a boat in deep water and while the angler may be fishing for a particular species it is quite possible he will land another kind of fish altogether. Off the Devon coast, the angler fish, better known as the fishing frog is occasionally taken when using live bait. It is a fearsome looking fish having a tremendous mouth. On top of its head are two long spines which wave about in the water and attract the fish. It grows to a good size.

RAY'S BREAM

Very few of these beautiful fish have been recorded as being taken on rod and line but there is always the chance that the novice might be successful where the seasoned angler has failed. The tail is shaped like that of the mackerel, the dorsal fin is long, starting from just behind the head. The anal fin is a third of the fish's length. The predominant colour is silver.

SEA CAT

Many years ago I was able to take a trip on a trawler and in the first haul there was a sea cat commonly known on the north-east coast as a wolf fish. It is aptly named for the teeth in its jaws are exceedingly powerful. It loves deep water and crabs for food. It has a large leathery dorsal fin and an anal fin which is half its length. The colour is dark grey and in the adult fish there are six or seven dark brown bands running from the back to the abdomen.

GAR-FISH

Known as the sea-pike this fish appears off the south-west and west coasts in April or May and remains in coastal waters until late autumn. It is easily identified by its very long jaws.

DRAGONET

A brilliantly coloured fish, it prefers deep water. Very slender built, it has two spiny dorsal fins and large ventral fins which are placed below the throat. It is occasionally caught when ledgering off the south coast.

SEA LAMPREY

This eel-like looking fish attacks other fish by fastening its suction mouth to their flanks and sucking their blood. A favourite prey is the salmon. However, it will go down in history as the fish that killed a king, the Royal personage being King Henry I, who history relates died from eating lampreys.

LUMP SUCKER

This species is fairly common off the west coast of Scotland and is taken when fishing among rock for pollack and coalfish. It has a suction device under its chin with which it fastens itself to rocks.

MYXINE

Wherever professional cod fishermen gather, conversation often centres round this fish which they call the borer. Worm-like in appearance it has the power of fastening on to a fish and boring into it. On one occasion on the North Shields fish quay I saw several cod which the myxine had attacked.

PIPE-FISH

Like the kangaroo this fish has a marsupial pouch in which the young are contained. I have never heard of one of these being taken by an angler, but on occasion they are taken by net-fishermen.

TORPEDO OR ELECTRIC RAY

Yet another strange fish is the torpedo ray which is able to generate enough electricity to stun the fish it has chosen as its prey.

CHAPTER X

CARE OF YOUR TACKLE

When fighting a fish everything depends on the skill of the angler and on the reliability of the tackle. I have known fishermen who were very careful about everyday things, but exceedingly lazy and careless over their fishing tackle after a day on the sea.

Rods, lines, reels, hooks, swivels and all the hundred-and-one other items that are included in the modern sea angler's equipment all need a little attention now and then. It is too late to think about putting varnish on a valuable split cane rod after the sea-water has got in and started to eat away the glue between the sections. Similarly it is no use expecting a reel to function smoothly if there is sand or dirt in the bearings or on the inside flange. Sand is one of the most abrasive mediums known to modern science.

We will assume that our fishing has been concluded for the year and we are faced with the task of checking and refurbishing the tackle. Of course there are little jobs that must be done at the end of every fishing expedition, but at the moment it is the annual inspection that is about to engage our attention.

Rods: Check every inch of each rod for fractures in the varnish and whippings. You will be surprised at the number you will find. These are mostly caused by carelessly putting the rod on rocks. If there are not too many scars on the varnish they can be patched up with a little slow-drying varnish. If the scratches are many it is a wise policy to strip the rod – take off the whippings and guides and remove the old varnish with varnish remover. The old method of using a razor blade is out of date and such a tool should only be used on spots that the remover will not shift.

Before taking off the guides measure the distance between each and jot it down in a note-book. This precaution ensures that they will be replaced in the same position and the balance of the rod retained. For split cane spinning rods this is most important, for a misplaced guide can spoil your casting. Of course you will still be able to cast with it but your distance will suffer. Remember the placing of the original guides by the rod-maker had been worked out along scientific lines so that casting would not be impaired and the stress of fighting a strong fish would be evenly distributed throughout the whole length of the rod.

After the rod has been stripped give it a light rub down with the finest glass paper, finishing off with a rub over with very fine steel wool. Never use too much muscle power when rubbing down, there is no need for it.

WAIT FOR A DRY DAY

When sure that all the old varnish has been removed and the rod is nice and smooth wait for a nice dry day for varnishing. The varnish will dry much quicker if the atmosphere has little or no moisture in it.

There are many cheap varnishes on the market – avoid them and pay the little extra for a good brand. Quick drying varnishes, when dry, are brittle and chip very easily, but slow drying do not.

You can put the varnish on with a brush but great care is needed to keep an even surface. Personally I use the index finger of my right hand as it gives a more even finish and the slight pressure you can apply gets the varnish into the cane or wood. To assist you when varnishing put a wood plug into the ferrule and to the plug screw in an eyed screw which can be slipped over another screw hook. (See sketch).

REVARNISHING A ROD

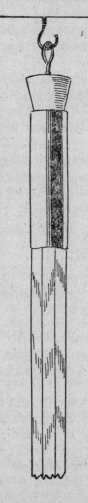

Screws

Wood Plug

Ferrule

Rod stripped ready for
first coat of varnish

When the job of varnishing is complete hang the rod sections in some place well out of the way of dust to dry. The drying process usually takes three or four days dependent on the humidity of the room. When satisfied that it is perfectly dry give the whole rod another light rub down with the steel wool, then put on your guides, spaced as per measurement in the note-book. When this is complete put on the whippings.

HOW TO WHIP A ROD

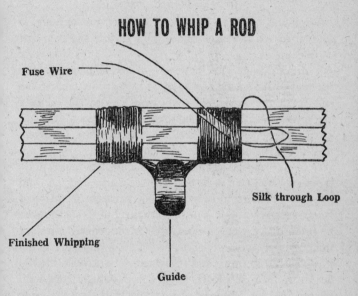

Fuse Wire

Silk through Loop

Finished Whipping

Guide

If you have never whipped a rod here's how. Purchase a 50-yard reel of rod tying silk, but be sure it is a lighter shade than what you require because when it is varnished it will go a shade darker unless you use colour preservative. Most rod whippings comprise six to eight turns of the silk with 20 or 30 for fastening the guides into position. If the original whippings numbered eight turns of silk each put on four then with a four inch length of the finest fuse wire form a loop and lay on top of the whipping and take the last four turns of the silk over the wire, put the end of the silk through the loop and pull the ends of the wire and the silk will vanish under the whipping and the end will be pulled through thus enabling you to cut it off with a razor blade close to the whipping. This method has the advantage over all other in that the whipping is kept tight all the time. A little Durofix rubbed on will close up any minute gap between the turns of silk.

When the whipping has been completed put on another coat of varnish and when this is dry a further and final coat completes.

There are some jobs, however, which should not be attempted by the amateur, but should be sent to a professional and one is the straightening of a rod. Occasionally, after a battle with a big fish on a light rod the top section will have a decided bend known as a "set". You can, of course, straighten it yourself, but in the case of a split cane rod unless you are very careful you can also ruin it. If you are determined to do the job yourself here is the best way. To get the rod back into line it is necessary to soften the glue between the strips of bamboo (cane). This is done by steaming, but great care must be taken that the steam doesn't enter the joints, because if this occurs the joints will open and your rod will be practically ruined. After steaming and straightening, and while the rod is still warm, it should be fastened to a straight edge until the glue has set. It is advisable to remove the guides before attempting the job.

If you take care of a rod there will be no need to strip it for at least five years, but a couple of coats of varnish in that period will help the rod to remain efficient.

If during the examination of the rod you think you have a loose ferrule it is an easy matter to test it. Fit the sections together and switch the rod back and forth as in casting, if the ferrule is not seating properly there will be felt a slight vibration at the joint. Loose ferrules are usually brought about through the cane or wood drying out over a number of years and if not attended to in the early stages will eventually lead to a fracture of the rod at that particular joint. Fibre glass rods suffer this as well.

LOOSE FERRULES

To repair a loose ferrule is not a difficult task to the handy man. If there is a pin through the ferrule into the wood use a small punch to ease it out a little and pull it out with pliers then apply a lighted match to that part of the ferrule which is over the wood. The heat will soften the glue and the ferrule can be pulled off. When it has been removed wrap the end of the wood with sewing silk or cotton depending on the amount of slackness, cover with ferrule cement and tap the ferrule back into position and when the cement has set replace the pin, but use a size larger. If the slackness is so pronounced that the above remedy will not cure it purchase a new set of ferrules and fit them.

If the cork handle of the rod looks dirty it can be made to look like new by giving it a rub down with steel wool upon which has been placed a few drops of acetone. This can be purchased from any chemist and a little will last years. In using it be careful it does not get on the rod or it will eat the varnish away. I always cover the rod near the handle before using the acetone, it is much safer.

One last thing before we pass on. Before putting the rods away give each one a rub down with wax polish. A waxed surface is easy to clean, dust doesn't stick to it as readily and also it can be wiped away with less effort. Most important thing in storing rods is to prevent moisture getting to the wood. A coating of wax can keep moisture (damp) out of those small cracks in a newly varnished rod that may develop anywhere, but seem most common at the point where the ferrule and rod meet.

REELS

Dirt and sand are the main enemies of all types of reels, and for this reason any reel you purchase should be so constructed that it can be dismantled at any time for cleaning. Most sea reels (excluding spinning) are made so that by nut the reel can be taken down quite easily and the ratchet mechanism examined.

Before examining the "works" give them a good cleaning with methylated spirits or petrol, if you have any, then when all the grease, dirt and sand has been removed examine closely the mechanism. If satisfied that all is in working order oil it before storage. On the other hand if a part shows any appreciable signs of wear and tear take it to an agent for that particular type of reel and have a new part fitted.

Multiplying and fixed spool reels are not so easily dealt with as there are more working parts all needing careful examination. A set of watchmaker's screwdrivers (three) with rotating tops are handy when dealing with multiplying reels as there are so many little screws. A good idea is to use a couple of saucers, one for the screws from the plate through which the spindle comes for the handle and the other for the screws of the other plate. This precaution will facilitate the work of assembling.

Clean all parts thoroughly as before, paying particular attention to the gears and the pawl and ratchet for these are the parts that suffer most if sand gets in.

In the fixed spool reel sand has a habit of getting in between the flange and the drum. Remove the drum taking care of the washers and screws and clean out all the old oil and grease. A good idea is to fill an enamel basin with meths., submerge the reel, minus drum, and turn the handle quickly a few times. This will shift those particles that stick in crevices. Dry and oil as before before putting together.

No matter what type of reel you have, reassemble it carefully. Screws should be tightened a little at a time, giving each screw a slight turn alternately and *the oil used should be of the best*, a poor grade will ruin the most expensive reel in a very short time.

LINES

The first thing to do is to take the lines off the reels and examine them for frayed sections because it is the line which connects you to the fish and on its strength when you go out next time depends whether you will have a chance of landing a fish.

The principal enemies of nylon lines are general deterioration due to long usage without attention and friction created through the line working through badly worn rings. Nylon monofilament also cracks if coiled badly and left so for a long period.

In a season's usage the most wear will be found to have taken place where the line is connected to the trace or other terminal tackle. The first foot of line should be most carefully looked over before storing and if in any doubt as to its fitness to stand another season's wear-and-tear it is far better to cut it off than to be sorry afterwards.

If the line is to remain unused for any length of time let it stay on the line-dryer until needed. The whole secret of keeping lines in tip-top condition is to store them so that the air can get to them. The line-dryer will accommodate several, but do not wind them on too tight, the more air that can get around the folds the better.

Of course, if you think a lot about your tackle, say for instance, as much as the writer does of his, you will dry your lines at the end of *each* fishing day and with such attention the most delicate and expensive line will last for years. If you are without a line-dryer the lines can be stored quite safely on a rolled newspaper. One last word, on no account let any line rest on corrosible metal for any length of time, to do so is a sure way of ruining it.

So much for ordinary sea lines. Some anglers prefer braided nylon for spinning and in this case a different process takes place before the line is fit for storing. In the first place if you can get some rain water it is a good idea to wash the line. Rain water is soft and is minus the chemicals in tap water, when thoroughly cleansed hang the line up to dry, but do not let it be exposed to excessive heat or sunlight. In the kitchen of my home I have fixed a couple of screws which have plastic covered hooks, purchased for a penny each and on these I put my braided lines and as they are fixed only a few inches from the ceiling the lines are enabled to dry without being subjected to excessive heat.

When absolutely sure that each line is perfectly dry they are taken down and coiled carefully on the line-dryer and stored in a cool place. Nylon lines are impervious to damp and mildew but that does not mean that they have to be treated rough. I give my lines just the same amount of care as I used to do when the material was silk and then when I want to use them again one has the satisfaction of knowing that the line is in perfect condition for battle.

TERMINAL TACKLE

Under this heading we have paternosters, ledgers, traces and ordinary casts. With the first-named, heat some lubricating oil and immerse the paternoster links in it, this bathing process will ensure that every link and swivel has been cleaned and oiled at the same time. On occasions swivels tend to rust and while oil will help them to function it will not delay the action of salt-water corrosion, therefore, if any swivel shows signs of rust renew them with bronze or stainless ones.

For several years my paternosters were of brass and bronze then stainless steel and now they are mostly plastic. The hooks are fastened to nylon, commonly called a snood or snead, the booms are made from quarter-inch perspex with nylon connecting each and at the end a swivel with which to fasten on the weight.

With such tackle it is an easy matter to clean it before putting away for the winter, after checking all knots.

With ledgers the first things to look at are the knots because this tackle is dragged over rocks and other abrasive obstacles and in a season's fishing the knots under such treatment are worn badly. If in doubt as to a knot's reliability cut it off and retie or else you will always have that uneasy feeling as to whether it will stand the strain.

Oil all swivels and examine for rust, and renew where necessary.

With ordinary nylon casts that have seen constant use for a season my method is to discard them and start with a fresh supply. Nylon is cheap enough these days for that.

The same goes for wire traces. After constant usage a wire trace develops little kinks, so instead of bothering to straighten these out, usually a long and tiresome task, it is far better to take off the swivels and make new ones. Once a trace has kinked it is never as strong again and should you get a kink in the same spot it is quite likely the wire will break, steel wire is particularly susceptible to this, Punjab, piano or elasticum wire will not stand too many kinks in the same place.

HOOKS

Take all hooks off tackles and after sharpening them put on a little vaseline to prevent rust setting in and then put them in a tin ready for being made up when needed.

CREEL OR BAG

If of wicker-work give it a good scrubbing with soap and water and hang out to dry and then put on a good coat of slow-drying varnish. The creel I use for estuary fishing has been in constant use for twenty years and is still serviceable.

With a bag, soap and water will get rid of any fishy smells, even if you have a detachable rubber or plastic inside it is always best to give the whole bag a good wash, for there is nothing more objectionable than a smell of stale fish.

Any leatherwork on bag or creel should be treated with leather preservative. Left to its own devices leather will dry out and rot in the course of time.

RUBBER BOOTS

These may be of the wader variety, hip length or knee-high boots but they all serve a definite purpose for the beach angler and should be checked frequently. Two of the chief enemies of rubber are sunlight and heat and any worn spot should be patched immediately and not left until it becomes a hole. After each fishing trip wash them thoroughly in clean water and they will retain their elasticity for years.

When storing rubber boots refrain from rolling or folding them, the folds will be the first place that will crack or wear through. Suspend the boots by the feet and not by the tops. A strong piece of cord placed over the instep and heel is an excellent way to hang them for then there is no strain on the rubber. These simple tasks will ensure long life for your boots and barring accidents will be the means of keeping your feet dry. Wet feet can often lead to bad colds and sometimes complications set in.

DAY TO DAY CARE OF TACKLE

After a day's fishing examine your rods for damage. If one of the guides is cracked renew it or it will ruin your line and may be the means of losing you a good fish. Give your rods a rub down with a clean cloth and then put on a little wax floor polish, finishing off with a nice easy rub down.

Check your reels for sand and if any has got in dismantle them, clean and oil.

Look over the line on each reel and test the last few inches and if in doubt about its fitness for another day cut it off. Always put your lines on the dryer after fishing. It is a simple matter to rewind them on to their respective reels the next day.

Examine your terminal tackle. Many anglers have bemoaned the fact that they have lost a fish through the tackle breaking, but I am convinced that nine times out of ten it has been their own fault. Wire kinks and nylon is considerably weakened through being frayed. Nylon will also crack and the only way to detect both frays and cracks is to examine the tackle when perfectly dry. Cracks are not so easy to detect, but if you examine them closely you may find a white mark. This is a crack and will sooner or later let you down.

The hooks on your tackles may have become dulled at the points, give them a rub over with a fine "stone". Or again you may have broken the barb off a hook in which case a new hook will have to be tied on. A touch of oil will assist your swivels to function better.

Always dry your net at the end of each outing or one of these days it will be so rotten that the bottom will fall out when you have a fish in it.

If your bag or creel has contained fish, dry it out and hang it up so that the air can get at the inside to take away the fishy smell.

None of these jobs take much time, but they are all well worth doing.

However, today, so far as rods are concerned, cane, steel and wood have been outdated by a modern material. I refer, of course, to fibre glass. Most sea rods nowadays are constructed from this, and the hints given previously apply also to fibreglass.

CHAPTER XI

TACKLE TINKERING

If one is fortunate enough to live near the sea the fishing will extend throughout the twelve months, but for those of us who are not in that category the only things left are memories and hope for the future.

During the winter months a profitable time can be spent tinkering with tackle. The amateur can, with a little time and patience, save himself quite a bit of money by making some of his tackle. For instance, it is quite an easy matter to construct the paternosters, ledgers or traces. We will take the paternoster first as it is the most used of any in beach or boat fishing.

To all intents and purposes we are now well advanced in the plastic age so the "pater" described is largely made of those materials.

You will need four feet of nylon monofilm of breaking strain depending upon the type of fish you hope to catch. All my paternosters are made with 20-pound nylon which is strong enough to tackle anything but the larger species like skate, conger, halibut or shark. You will also require two swivels, one having a link, six beads of brown or green colour no bigger than a sweet pea seed, three pieces of perspex half-an-inch wide and a quarter of an inch thick and a drill. The drill is used to make a hole for the nylon to run through and also holes for the snoods.

Put your link swivel on first and then three inches away tie a simple knot and thread on a bead followed by the first boom. A bead is then threaded to rest on the top of the boom and another knot is tied. The snood suspending from this boom will rest on the bottom and will be just right to capture flat fish.

MAKING A PLASTIC THREE-BOOM PATERNOSTER

Line swivel

Ordinary Knot

Wood Bead

Perspex Boom
3½in. to 4in. long

Boom Thickness ¼in

Hole for Snood

Hole for Nylon

Nine Inches

Overall
Length
3ft.

Eight inches

Large Link Swivel
for weight

CONSTRUCTING TWO-HOOK LEDGER

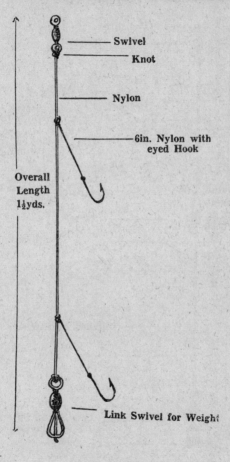

Swivel

Knot

Nylon

6in. Nylon with eyed Hook

Overall Length 1½yds.

Link Swivel for Weight

MAKING A TRACE FOR SPINNING

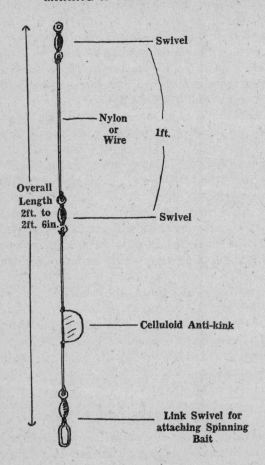

Swivel

Nylon
or
Wire

1ft.

Overall
Length
2ft. to
2ft. 6in.

Swivel

Celluloid Anti-kink

Link Swivel for
attaching Spinning
Bait

The next boom is eight inches away and the third nine inches away. The top swivel is tied on and your paternoster is complete, and should measure about three feet long.

For a two-hook ledger a five-foot length of nylon is needed, two long-shanked sea hooks and two swivels, one of which must have a swivel link for the weight. Tie on the bottom swivel first and nine inches up fasten on your first hook to the main nylon with a nine-inch piece of monofilm. The second hook is tied on 18 inches higher up, the top swivel is put on and the ledger is complete. (See drawing on page 139.)

To make a trace for spinning or live baiting for the big fish you need at least three swivels. A link, one at the bottom for the spinner or the live bait tackle, another half-way up and one for the top. For a spinning trace an anti-kink is needed if you use a braided line, but it is not necessary if the line is of monofilm. To allow for making the knots a three feet length of nylon or wire is used. (See drawing on page 140).

Once you have made a few of these tackles you will be able to vary the spacing of the hooks, etc., to suit the requirements of the day. Always take a few extra tackles with you, because on occasions you may be dogged by bad luck and lose some on rocks, which is often the case when fishing for conger and pollack.

(See drawing on page 139.)

(See drawing on page 140).

KEEPING THEM TIDY

The snoods one uses for paternosters if kept together have a habit of becoming so entangled that valuable fishing time is wasted in getting them parted. To avoid this is simple for all you have to have is a snood holder, but your snoods should all be the same length. If you have different lengths of nylon or wire snoods you will want several, so to avoid this I make my snoods in three sizes, and have constructed a holder for each size. The sizes are six inches, eight and nine inches.

The holder is made this way. Visit a junk shop and purchase an old bamboo curtain rail; if unable to find one ordinary bamboo of three inches diameter will do. Cut a piece a quarter of an inch longer than the snood, thus for nine-inchers the bamboo would be nine and a quarter inches. Next, using a hand-saw cut a number of slots a quarter of an inch down the bamboo then over the tongues the loops of the snoods can be placed. At the other end glue in a ring of felt or cork against which the bend of the hook will rest. Two corks, one for either end, will keep everything quite ship-shape and there will be no danger of torn fingers or hands from bare hooks and what is more the snood will be kept perfectly straight. The idea is not mine, but is one that I picked up many years ago when fishing off the Florida coast, U.S.A.

Of course if the bamboo is of a large diameter larger corks will be required. A friend of mine uses snood holders made from Spanish reed because it is much lighter than bamboo, the only fault I have to find with the material is that it is not so durable.

FOR SAFETY

For artificial baits it is a good idea to protect the hook points against accident, personal and otherwise. An ordinary cork from a wine bottle can be cut into three discs. Cut a sixteenth of an inch slit in a disc from the outside to the centre, smoothing off with fine glass paper. The shank of the hook is put through the slit and the disc of cork is impaled on the hooks. Simple, but quite effective, for it prevents all those tangles you always get when there are a lot of treble-hooked baits in a box.

BAMBOO SNOOD HOLDER

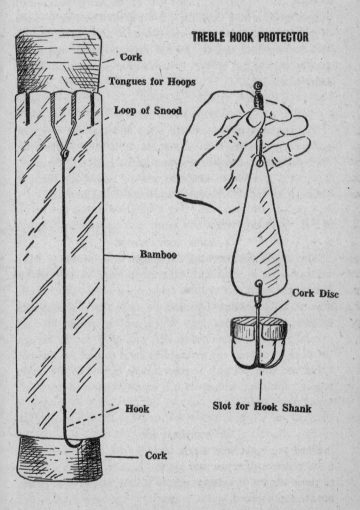

TREBLE HOOK PROTECTOR

Cork

Tongues for Hoops

Loop of Snood

Bamboo

Hook

Cork

Cork Disc

Slot for Hook Shank

ROD REST

For the beach angler a rod-rest is an important piece of his equipment. Three years ago I discarded my wooden rest for a metal one which was made out of an Army tank aerial picked up in a junk shop for a few pence. The fork is made of heavy gauge copper wire, then covered with rubber tubing and is fixed into the top of the first section of the aerial The bottom of this section is flattened and then filed in the shape of a spear.

CLEANING SPOONS

The spinning enthusiast will often find that the action of salt-water on metal baits sometimes dulls their polish with the result that their power of attraction is considerably reduced. They can be made to look like new by immersing them in tomato juice and polishing with a piece of chamois.

A HANDY LINE - DRYER

The angler who likes to travel light will invariably leave his line dryer at home and will trust to being able to dry his line on the back of a chair or some other object that is suitable. A first-class line-dryer can be made out of a couple of wooden spring clothes pegs which can be bought at most general stores for a few pence. All you have to do is clip the pegs on to your rod several feet apart so thet the line can be wound over them. The pegs can be carried in the tackle bag or pocket and with them it is an easy matter to dry a line at any time.

MAKING A ROD

After you have been tackle tinkering for a few years it is quite possible that you will get the urge to make a rod and in these days it is a fairly simple matter as rod fittings can now be purchased quite reasonably. Quite a number of tackle makers are producing parcels in which are the component parts for making a rod. By making your own you save several pounds and in addition have the satisfaction of having built it yourself. The author's son uses a boat rod he made himself from such a parcel.

In Devon and Cornwall many of the locals use rods they have made themselves out of bamboo, which can be bought for a few pence. The cane is straightened with the aid of heat, usually a gas flame in which the cane is turned by hand slowly, and when heated it can be straightened. The canes they use are the male because the female has unsightly grooves near the nodes (leaf joints) and as a result is not so strong.

After straightening, the nodes are smoothed down with fine glass paper and the canes are given a good rub with coarse steel wool so that they will take the stain or varnish. Unless this is done it is nearly impossible to get the cane stained or varnished due to the skin of the cane which has a lacquer-like surface.

Corks for the handle can be obtained from most tackle shops and when glued in position can be shaped with a file, finishing off with glass paper. Reel fittings can also be obtained at most tackle stores. By this method it is possible to make a good rod for as little as a pound or two, the dearest item being the top section which can be fibre glass or split cane. In building a rod you need quite a bit of time not forgetting the patience.

CHEAP SPINNERS

Spinning natural baits can be quite expensive should you be unlucky enough to lose a few spinners and quite early on in the writer's angling career the method of making spinners was learned. The items needed are celluloid, the best thickness being .045, some brass wire, swivels and some lead wire. The tools required are two, a pair of sharp scissors for cutting the

CONSTRUCTING A SPINNER

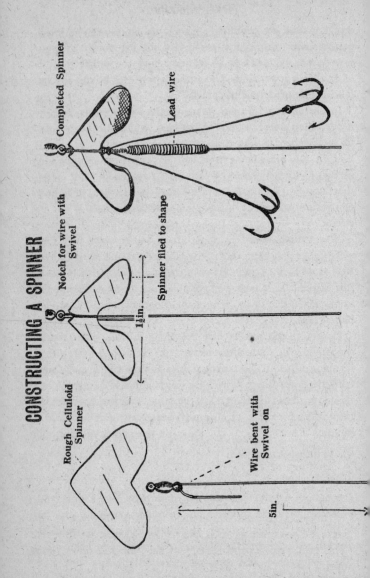

Rough Celluloid Spinner

Wire bent with Swivel on

5in.

Notch for wire with Swivel

Spinner filed to shape

1½in.

Completed Spinner

Lead wire

celluloid and a fine file for shaping the spinner. In addition, steam from a boiling kettle will be needed to bend the celluloid so that it acts like a propellor when being reeled in.

If you study the sketches little difficulty should be experienced. After the bent wire, complete with swivel, has been put in position over the notch at the head of the spinner twist the short end of the wire round the long piece, commencing the twisting process close to the celluloid. When this is done it will have tightened the spinner into position and it is now ready to be treated with steam which will soften the celluloid and make it pliable so that it can be shaped. As soon as you have put the twist on the spinner plunge it into cold water and the twists will stay put. You now have a spinner.

To put on the hooks you can use nylon or wire depending on what you propose to use it for; if conger, use wire which can be put on before you twist the spinner into position or after just as you choose. The way I do it is thread the hook wire through the wire which holds the spinner into position as it is an easy matter to push it through between the celluloid and wire and a couple of twists will make it secure. The wire for one hook should be a little shorter than the other so that it can hold the hook into the belly or shoulder of the bait while the second hook being on a longer piece will be near the tail of the bait. The lead wire is twisted on and your work is finished. If you want the lead wire to be a permanent job run a little solder over it.

TO KEEP REELS CLEAN

To keep your reels free of sand and dirt when not in use make a canvas bag for each and to the bag fit a zip fastener. This need not cost much but may save the cost many times over.

The items mentioned are only a few of the things that an

angler can do and so enjoy himself when unable to fish. Tackle tinkering is interesting and quite good fun particularly during those long winter nights when one is apt to get bored with the humdrum things of life.

CHAPTER XII

IN FOREIGN WATERS

It is many years since sea fishing became one of the international sports. It was brought about by the kindness of a Boston (U.S.A.) sportsman, Alton B. Sharp, who presented a beautiful and valuable trophy to be fished for by two teams, one representing the United States and the other the British Empire. Since then other countries have sent teams.

The event is called the "The International Tuna Angling Cup Match" and it is fished in Lobster Bay, Wedgeport, Nova Scotia, Canada. The teams fish for three days, twelve hours a day. In these waters giant tuna of 500 lb. to 700 lb. are taken fairly regularly. The 1951 match saw the British Empire Team win with a total of 2,039 points. The points are allocated on a basis of one point per lb., with additional points for the biggest number of fish caught and also for the largest fish taken. In the 1951 match the United States team came second with a couple of large fish. One weighed 737 lb. and the other 716 lb.

The principal bait is a herring which is trolled and is attached to a powerful wire trace.

By a stroke of luck I happened to be in Wedgeport at the first match where a gale was blowing. So bad did conditions become that at the end of fifteen hours' fishing the competition ended. With the score standing at 9-3 the British team was declared the winner and so ended the first international. Since then, excluding the war years and the three or four years that both countries needed to get back to normal the international has been fished.

The tuna is only one of the many sea giants that roam the waters lapping the American continent and to mention only a few there are *Marlin* (Black Pacific), *Marlin* (blue), *Marlin* (silver), *Marlin* (striped) and *Marlin* (white). *Sailfish* (Atlantic), *Sawfish*, *Tarpon*. The above can be classed as the heavyweights but there are also fish which can be ranked in the dreadnought class, namely the sharks and *Manta Ray* (devil fish).

In addition there are several hundred other species of fish to lure the angler to America for sport.

FISHERMAN'S PARADISE

For several years it was my good fortune to be in the U.S.A. and during that time every spare moment was spent in fishing, and while the writer has pleasant memories among the tuna and marlin, his greatest thrills were when fishing for tarpon and bonefish in Florida when a guest of his brother, the Rev. Dr. S. H. Davies of Miami.

There is no under-estimating Florida seas as a fisherman's paradise, for I feel fairly safe in saying that few places in the world offer such a variety of game fish.

My brother and I had tired of fishing for bass in Lake Okeechobee and thought we would give the Gulf Stream a try. According to the local newspapers, fishing had been pretty good at Key Largo and Tavernier.

We arrived at Key Largo as the stars in the blue summer night were beginning to fade. Wakened birds were twittering in the branches. A grey mist was rising, and in the air was the fresh, damp smell of early morning. Lights appeared here and there in the dusky landscape, and down the silent road came the "chug-chug" of rubber boots as dark, clumsy-gaited figures made for the beach. Lanterns bobbed about the cluster of fish houses, and the creak of thole-pins and the plash of oar blades indicated that other fishermen were out.

In the blue haze over the ocean hung the dim shapes of boats with sails set, running for the fishing grounds. The little noises of preparation, the grating of a keel on the wet shingle, the dip of oars, and the lapping of waves against the boats only completed the great, cool, damp silence of the morning. And the salt tang in the air was very good to smell.

After a delicious breakfast of turtle steaks we went down to the beach, and within ten minutes had hired a motor launch complete with guide – a woman – as clever and reliable a "boatman" as the best. Chatting with our guide I gathered that one unfamiliar with Gulf Stream fishing might gain the impression that only rich people are able to enjoy the thrills of landing a sailfish, tarpon, marlin or tuna. That was undoubtedly true a few years ago, but today it is within the means of most. A Britisher who is able to visit Florida will find that he will be welcomed wherever he goes. Local anglers are ever willing to help with information as to the best locations and baits. Living conditions will meet the requirements of the most fastidious. No dirt and smoke from industry, but always the fresh, clean, smell of salt air.

Well, for a start we tried sea-trout fishing in a couple of sounds, many of which are found around the northern end of Key Largo. Gold devons and spoons proved quite good, and after taking half a dozen we decided to move off to deeper water and try our luck with barracuda. Trolling a small mackerel, my brother was soon fast to a nice one, and after a ten minute battle brought him to gaff. His weight was 8 lb. This was the first of several we took before lunch, the largest being 10 lb. The ten-pounder put up a tough fight and gave me quite a few thrills before the gaff was slipped home.

Immediately after lunch we got cracking again and secured a really fine mixed bag including jack, snapper, grouper, yellowtail and barracuda. The strike of the 'cuda is hard and the fight sustained, usually right up to the boat; and if the tackle is light the angler has quite a lot of fun when the hook goes home, as invariably the fish leaps into the air time and time again. In appearance they are like our fresh-water pike but their teeth are much larger. They are just as good eating as they are gamesters.

SEEKING THE BONEFISH

However, our best sport was not among the large fish but with an opponent that is now being publicized as the gamest of all the smaller fish in either salt or fresh water. Although my knowledge of the bonefish is limited, the sport we had prompts me to agree. For speed and stamina I doubt that any fish of the same approximate weight can even approach the bonefish, while the method of angling for this species is as interesting as dry-fly fishing for the wariest of trout. The bonefish seldom leaps from the water when hooked, but if the angler does succeed in getting the barb set into a five-pounder he will think he is tied to a streak of lightning!

Bonefish inhabit the flats, and on the fourth day of my visit I had an opportunity of testing their mettle. The placid mangrove shores surrounded us, giving the impression of a fresh-water lake rather than tidal waters. A pelican flapped his laborious way across the cove. A flock of ducks whirred down the bay. Then came a splash on the edge of the flat. The bonefish were moving. Our guide pointed to a commotion just off the edge of the mangroves – a school of bonefish feeding with the advancing tide.

I was using a 5 ft. 6 in. steel casting rod, Hardy Altex No. 3 reel and, for bait, a small hermit crab. My offering was placed in front of the school. There was a light crab-like touch, and I struck – but too late. Several times more the same scene was repeated, and my respect and admiration for the bonefish grew. Then unexpectedly my strike went home and in the twinkling of an eye, over 100 ft. of 6 lb. nylon monofilm line had gone rushing out through the guides. The fish's speed slackened, and for the next five minutes it was give and take. The fight lasted twelve minutes and I thought my capture would be at least 10 or 12 lb. However, when Harry (my brother) swung him aboard with the net he was only a little fellow, 5 lb. 2 oz.

We had two days among the bonefish, and, believe me they stand out in my memory. The bonefish will give you something unobtainable in any other form of fishing; nor will the silver-and-white warriors suffer by comparison with larger and more famous game fish. The bonefish is useless for food, so we released them to provide sport for other anglers, including perhaps *you*.

TARPON FISHING

Twelve months later I was again in Florida. A hard winter's work in New York in which strife had been more severe than I ever remembered it before, found me as my, friend Dr. Samual Gelband expressed it, "Not sick, but somewhat out of health."

Only one thing would prevent me going to pieces and that was a quiet and lengthy holiday, preferably by the sea. Two days later I was on the train for Florida.

On arrival at my brother's vicarage it was a pleasant surprise to learn that he had fixed up for a couple of day's tarpon fishing.

Imagine a herring, six, or seven feet long and weighing anything between one and two hundredweight. Cover this creature with scales, each as large as four 10p pieces and shining like newly-burnished silver. Endow it with the strength of a steel spring and the speed of a motor-boat, then you may obtain some faint idea of this splendid game fish – the tarpon, known among Florida sportsmen as the "silver king".

In many of the tidal rivers small tarpon of ten to twenty pounds can be taken on the fly-rod with large gaudy flies and on the spinning rod with spoons and plugs, but for the really big chaps you have to use a boat on the high sea.

To cut a long story short, we stayed in the town of Homestead and during the two days we had with the tarpon we hooked six but only boated a couple. For bait a mullet is the best, while the trace is of wire to withstand the chaffing of the tarpon's teeth.

My brother hooked the first one and in one tremendous rush over one hundreds yards of line was out and up out of the sea into the dazzling sunshine leapt a huge fish, more like a column of living silver than anything else, wonderful and terrifying to see. The fish shook his head fiercely, but the hook held. With the butt of his rod in the cup of the harness he was wearing, Harry worked him near and then up in the air went the silver king again and this time the hook flew out.

The other three we lost regained their freedom in a similar fashion, the two we landed were each over 80 lb., small as tarpon go, but the fight mine gave me was quite enough to be going on with. Our guide told us that the main enemy of the tarpon is the shark and many an angler can bear this out for on numerous occasions when the tarpon is being brought alongside the boat a shark has rushed in and torn it off the hook.

Most of the guides will provide harness and tackle so should you be contemplating a visit to the domain of the "silver king" don't bother to take tackle, for in all probability it would be useless for this kind of fishing.

STRIPED BASS

This fish is a larger edition of our own splendid gamester

– the sea bass and is much sought after for food. It is essentially a surf fisherman's species and one of the finest places I know to engage him in battle is San Francisco.

'Frisco is almost surrounded by water, and bass are caught on both the ocean side of the city and in the bay. The ocean fishing starts in June and continues to November. Fishing at Baker's Beach in the Golden Gate starts in May and in other parts along the beach it opens in July. Striped bass fishing appeals to the ladies equally with the men and, on more than one occasion, members of the fair sex have won trophies offered by the various clubs and associations.

Some of the best "Striper" fishing is to be had in the northern part of San Francisco Bay. The bay is shallow and one can fish it either from the shore or from almost any mark at which a boat is anchored.

Within reasonable reach by either train or car, there is literally more sporting water than a man could fish in a long lifetime. I found when there that the majority of American anglers return week after week to their favourite haunts.

Some of the largest fish are taken trolling spoon or red-headed plugs with white bodies which seem to be the most popular. No sinker is used in shallow water but, in the deeps, leads weighing a pound or more are needed. Some anglers use a terminal tackle which drops the lead when a fish strikes and is hooked, so that they get the full benefit of its sporting capabilities. Sardines about a foot long are used as natural bait. I noticed that each angler appeared to have his own method of cutting his bait and attaching it to the hooks which vary from 6/o to 10/o, The lines run from 6 to 12 thread and as in American fishing circles a thread represents 2-lb. breaking strain it is an easy matter to compute the strength of a line. Almost any reel will do providing it has a good line capacity, but the reel most in evidence was a reel with a brake and holding 200 yards of line.

The rods for surf (beach) fishing are of the spring butt

type, the tips of which are about 7 ft. long. But for boat fishing they use a rod about half the weight of a "spring butt", the tip of which weighs approximately six ounces for its six feet length, the butt apart. A wire trace is essential.

Some idea of the number of fish caught every year at this angling paradise can be gleaned from the fact that about 100,000 people take out licenses in the Bay district alone. In the size the fish range from 6 lb. to 30 lb. although an occasional 40-pounder is landed.

For years the San Francisco Striped Bass Club in conjunction with the Associated Sportsmen of California fought for the protection of the "Striper", but it was only in comparatively recent years that laws were passed prohibiting the commercial netting and sale of striped bass; as a result of which the fishing has much improved. Now, except for an off-day, which is a rare occurrence, a man can be astir at five or six o'clock in the morning, go to the nearest beach or pier, get his limit of five bass over twelve inches long and be at work by nine.

On Sundays, when trolling is good, hundreds of boats can be seen over marks where the run is on.

Anyone who contemplates combining a business trip to these parts with sport, should communicate with the Associated Sportsmen, Pacific Building, Market Street, San Francisco, U.S.A., which is the headquarters of the Striped Bass Association.

Other sporting species that a visiting angler can expect to catch include Bonito, Cero Mackerel, King Mackerel, Spanish Mackerel, Cobia, Wahoo, Red Snapper, Mangrove Snapper, Yellowtail, Red Grouper and Snook.

IN CANADIAN WATERS

In Canada there is good fishing all round the coastline and

the visitor is well catered for in the way of boats, tackle, etc. The sea anglers of Canada are a fine lot and a stranger is soon made to feel at home. Most of the species found in the colder waters of the U.S.A. are there and while there is a good deal of boat fishing most fishing is done from rocks and beaches. At the mouths of many of the rivers large salmon are taken in the open sea with rod, line and spinner.

At Cape Breton, Nova Scotia, a big industry has been built up around the Broadbill Swordfish. A fleet of over 300 power boats have their headquarters in the port of Glace Bay and for thrills there is nothing to equal a trip with one of these large boats in search of the giant sword-fish. They are rarely caught with rod and line but it is exciting to see the harpooner standing in his "nest" in the bowsprits waiting to launch his weapon at a broadbill as it cruises just below the surface. Of course, if you fancy hiring a boat to go after these monsters, usual weight 500 lb., there is nothing to stop you, providing you have the cash.

Tuna are also plentiful in Canadian waters, but before you embark on a trip for these game fish be sure you are in the pink of condition because you never know how long the battle will last. Even a small tuna of 300 lb. will fight for three hours or more while the really big chaps of seven and eight hundred pounds will keep you busy for ten or twelve hours. To those anglers with even a slight touch of heart trouble take my advice and leave this kind of fishing alone. The thrills are all right but the reaction is not so good. The last battle I was engaged in with one put me in hospital for three weeks with a badly wrenched shoulder and fractured wrist not to speak of serious burns on both hands. That was over 20 years ago and while rods and reels have improved a great deal since then I never want to tangle with another tuna.

Of Canadian fishing there is, however, one memory that

stands out above all others. It was the occasion I landed a large *Tyee*, commonly known as a chinook or royal salmon. These giant salmon, fish of over 100 lb. are on record, are fished for by trolling and are quite common all round the Canadian coast.

The place where my first royal salmon was caught was a little bay about thirty miles from Vancouver. The boat was anchored in about 30 ft. of water, for a companion I had a journalist friend who was a dyed-in-the-wool tyee fisherman. I watched the old-timers in a couple of boats nearby to see how they set about the job. The first thing that caught my attention was the tackle used; a short, stout casting rod, heavy reel, extra stout cuttyhunk line. We had come prepared with an ample supply of wire traces, spoons, devons and weights, etc., but I looked at my salmon spinning rod and Altex No. 3 reel with dismay. How could they stand the strain of the heavy weight that was needed to get the bait down. Jack Coulson (my friend) had a powerful short rod and large free-running, centre-pin reel loaded with 30-lb. line.

Swish! the line went through the air. Plump, the weight and spoon landed in the water as far as the light rod would allow me to fling the combination of a six-inch heavy silver and gold spoon and six ounces of lead. And then they were slowly retrieved. Cast after cast was made and the minutes wagged into hours and still no fish would come to bite. At length I made a beautiful cast. I started to reel in the 15-lb. silk line when the rod was nearly torn from my hands. I sent up a prayer to the inventor of the fixed spool reel ... A thrill went over me. "I've got him!" I shouted. But just as Jack turned to see what I had the line slackened – and I reeled in the remnants of my wire trace. The fish had twisted the wire and snapped it.

Well-nigh exhausted by lunch-time I was sitting in the boat, resting, when Jack turned to me with a knowing grin. He never said a word; but I followed his eye to his line.

It was taut and his reel was beginning to turn. Then it fairly whizzed off the drum with Jack braking it with a leather thumb guard.

"He's got one!" I heard several other anglers shout and I was far more excited than the more experienced and stolid Jack, who was playing the fish. Back and forth the line went. Now the line would rush out through the rings as the frightened, maddened fish made a desperate effort to excape. Now Jack was reeling in slowly and cautiously as the fish relaxed his fight. He was close to the boat by this time, and I was ready with the gaff. "Ready," shouted my companion. "Let him have it." The big grey body loomed up beside the boat, the gaff sank home and 32 lb. of Royal Chinook came aboard.

After removing the spoon we gloated over the prize. When we looked up several other anglers were battling. While we watched, ten salmon were boated, including a 45-lb. fish by a young woman.

Once more our offerings were sent out and this time it was my turn to land a fish, but he was only a baby of 14 lb. This concluded our catch for the day, but fourteen hours later we were back again and our luck was in for we anchored, or so it seemed, in a shoal of large and hungry salmon. In six hours we landed five between us. My best fish was a 49-pounder which Jack beat with a 52-lb. fish and followed up shortly afterwards with another 50-pounder.

It is the memory of the one hour and twenty minutes' fight I had with my fish that I refer to. He knew every trick in the book and a lot more besides and but for the fact that I was using a more powerful rod and reel than the previous day I am sure the fish would have won.

On 7th August, 1941, Mrs. T. B. Randall of Vancouver became champion of the Tyee Club with a fish of 66½ lb. It is interesting to note that one of the founder members of this club was a British colonel, whose name I have forgotten.

Unlike our old friend the Atlantic salmon, the Royal Chinook, both male and female, die after spawning and I have seen thousands floating downstream tail first, dead or dying from a fungoid growth which attacks them in their weakened state after spawning.

With hook and line, a well-anchored boat, a propitious day, and good luck, there is no salmon fishing to compare with fishing for a Royal Chinook. It is indeed royal sport with a royal quarry. The only fault I have to find is that the flesh of this gamester is not such good eating as our own salmon.

AUSTRALIA

The national sport of this country has for some years now been cricket, but in the last fifteen years angling has been running a close second. Notwithstanding the immense number of sharks that must be fed, the sea teems with fish.

The whiting is well represented along the coasts where it delights to poke about the sandy shores just outside the long line of breakers. It is mostly caught with rod and line from beach and rocks. It attains a size a little larger than we are accustomed to meet in our waters.

The most common of all the smaller Australian species and those most caught are the mullets. Next to the mullets in quantity are bream and blackfish, but the fish most sought for is undoubtedly the schnapper.

The home of this species is in the deep sea, generally a considerable distance from the shore and in the neighbourhood of a shelving reef. The bait is usually the flesh of a fresh mullet and the tackle a three-hook paternoster.

Most of the Australian fish are brilliantly coloured and their dorsal fins have sharp spines which can inflict a nasty wound on the unwary angler.

It is questionable though whether the excellent fishing in

Australian waters would ever have been publicized but for the giant fish that inhabit these areas such as marlin, shark, etc.

NEW ZEALAND

In recent years the coastal waters of these islands have been in the news a great deal following some fine catches of marlin, sailfish, sharks and numerous small game fish. I have never had the pleasure of fishing these waters, but several of my friends have and they all consider the fishing rivals that of anywhere in the world. A sweeping statement, but then most anglers use flowery language when they experience good sport and as these waters are in their infancy, so far as angling with rod and line is concerned, it is quite possible.

In common with the growth of the sport many hotels now cater for anglers and hire out tackle and arrange parties under qualified guides and seamen.

From what I have been told it appears that the best all-round sport is had during the months of February and March.

SOUTH AFRICA

Many of the species which inhabit American waters are also found off the coasts of South Africa. There are sharks, yellowtail, manta, snook, skate and numerous others. The sport is fairly well organised and a visitor can hire tackle at most places for quite a small fee. Beach and rock fishing is much practised by the locals and the tackle used is similar to that which we use in this country, indeed, most of the tackle dealers sell equipment made in this country. Information is available on the type of fishing in a particular place at Government offices.

Of course there are many other countries that can and do provide facilities for the sea angler, but they are far too numerous to deal with here in the space at my disposal.

In fishing foreign waters the same general principles of angling operate. The tackle for big game fish may be slightly different in outward appearance, but once a fish is hooked, whether it be pygmy or giant the battle is much the same, and so with air travel being speeded up year after year the writer can visualize the time when there will be a regular flow of anglers from this country to those places where the sport is of the highest. As I see it, what better ambassadors could there be than anglers from one country to another?

CHAPTER XIII

RECORD FISH

Occasionally an angler is lucky enough to land a fish which tops the existing record. I use the word occasionally advisedly because on looking through the records it is seen that many have stood for years.

The period which saw many records broken was that between 1933 and 1940. In those seven years seven new records were set up.

The country which I think will surprise everyone in the near future by providing several new records is Scotland. At the moment so far as sea fishing is concerned it is more or less an unknown quantity. I have visited the west coast on numerous occasions and have never been disappointed and, what is more, while there, have seen the net fisherman land fish, whiting, mackerel, pollack and coalfish that would have smashed the records.

Why is it that so few sea anglers visit Scotland? The answer is not far to seek. Accommodation is very limited and unless one has a car considerable difficulty is experienced in getting from place to place. It would take millions of pounds to put in a good transport system to cover all the villages and hamlets and connect them with the towns. Take Shieldaig in Ross-shire for instance, where the record whiting was caught. You take the train from Inverness to Strathcommon and from there you journey the twenty-one miles by a bus, the prime business of which is to carry mails. That bus runs once a day. When you get to Shieldaig it is a case of "Shanks' pony" to get to the other villages. So in my humble opinion, for some years to come the west coast of Scotland will remain the best area for prospecting anglers because it is not over fished and there are still many places that can be classed as virgin.

In regard to records, many changes have been made in the last two years, by the British Record (Rod-caught) Fish Committee. Those records not authenticated have been removed from the list.

Now for the records:

WEIGHT	ANGLER	PLACE	YEAR
	Bass		
18 lb. 12 ozs.	Mr. F. Borley	Felixtowe	1943
	Black Bream		
6 lb. 7 ozs.	J. L. Atkins	Devon	1973
	Brill		
16 lb.	Mr. C. H. Fisher	Isle of Man	1950
	Bull Huss		
21 lb. 3 ozs.	Mr. J. Holmes	Looe	1955
	Coalfish		
30 lb. 12 ozs.	A. F. Harris	Eddystone	1973
	Cod		
53 lb.	G. Martin	Devon	1972

WEIGHT	ANGLER	PLACE	YEAR
	Conger		
102½ lb.	Mr. B. Thomson	Mevagissey, Cornwall	1974
	Dab		
2lb. 12 ozs.	A. B. Hare	Skerries	1968
	Flounder		
5 lb. 11 ozs.	Mr. A. G. L. Cobbledick	Fowey	1956
	Gurnard		
11 lb. 7¼ ozs.	Mr. C. W. King	Wallasey	1952
	Haddock		
12 lb. 10 ozs.	K. P. White	Manacles	1975
	Hake		
25 lb. 5 ozs.	Mr. H. W. Steele	Belfast	1962
	Halibut		
197 lb.	J. Newman	Pentland Firth	1974
	John Dory		
10 lb. 12 ozs.	B. L. Perry	Porthallow, Cornwall	1963

WEIGHT	ANGLER	PLACE	YEAR
	Ling		
50 lb. 8 ozs.	Mr. B. M. Coppen	Eddystone	1974
	Mackerel		
5 lb. 6 ozs.	S. Beasley	Eddystone Lighthouse	1969
	Grey Mullet		
10 lb. 1 oz.	Mr. P. C. Libby	Portland	1952
	Plaice		
7 lb. 15 ozs.	B. Brodie	Salcombe	1964
	Pollack		
25 lb.	R. J. Hosking	Eddystone	1972
	Pouting		
5 lb. 8 ozs.	R. S. Armstrong	Berry Head	1969
	Red Bream		
9 lb. 8 ozs.	B. H. Reynolds	Cornwall	1974
	Common Skate		
214 lb.	J. A. E. Olsson	Scapa Flow	1968

WEIGHT	ANGLER	PLACE	YEAR
	Sole		
4 lb. 3 ozs.	R. Wells	Redcliffe	1974
	Tope (male)		
62 lb.	Mr. D. S. Southcombe	Weymouth	1946
	Tope (female)		
74 lb. 11 ozs.	Mr. A. H. Harris	Caldy Island	1964
	Tunny		
851 lb.	Mr. L. Mitchel Henry	Whitby	1933
	Turbot		
31 lb. 4 ozs.	P. Hutchings	Eddystone	1972
	Whiting		
6 lb. 3 ozs.	Mrs. R. Barrett	Cornwall	1971
	Ballen Wrasse		
7 lb. 10 ozs.	B. K. Lawrence	Cornwall	1971

CHAPTER XIV

CAMPING AND FISHING

Fortunate indeed is the angler who has a car, for then he can combine with his fishing one of the finest pastimes of all – that of living out-of-doors. For years I have held the opinion that the best way to get the most out of a fishing weekend or holiday is to include a tent in the equipment. Many of the best angling spots around our coasts lie well off the beaten track and in these what I term "Santuaries of Silence" a tent is a necessity.

Broadly speaking camping is an art – the art of living comfortably outdoors without the conveniences of home. It is not, and need not be "roughing it" as many people believe. Under certain conditions camping can be rugged, but if common sense is used it can at most times be a pleasant change.

Climatic conditions must be given some thought and a good rule is to select equipment to meet the worst weather. However, the most important thing on a camping holiday in which one is moving from place to place is to select good sites for pitching the tent. No doubt you have heard what a camp site ought to include and I won't add very much more – dry land, no fly pests, plenty of sun but not too much and no danger of falling tree limbs. Yet here's a detail you might overlook, dry land is not necessarily a matter of altitude. A patch on top of a mountain can be wet and a patch in the lowlands dry. The particular spot of land is what usually counts.

A stretch of flat ground is not as flat as it looks. Close examination discloses undulations. The high spots may be only two or three inches higher than the hollows, but if your tent is perched on one of these you may find yourself on dry ground after a downpour when the rest of the locality is sodden.

As to avoidance of winged pests many campers take the wise precaution of keeping away from swampy areas and rank vegetation where these terrors breed. Yet you can camp on open ground and be overridden by flies; that is if there happens to be a line of vegetation running from a stream to your camp site. On the other hand if you are separated from the water by some dry, open land the chances are you will live a fairly flyless life. Many details such as these are worth a camper's investigation.

THE BEST

What is the best frontage? That is the first question after you have chosen a decent site and are ready to pitch the tent. Local topography and weather conditions supply about nine-tenths of the answer. In a valley for example, prevailing winds tend to blow either up or down the valley. Pitch your tent with either its rear or side to the wind. On the other hand if your site is a small open patch surrounded by woods it may not matter how the tent faces.

Beware of sudden storms in the case of an exposed site. Speaking of storms, the condition of various holding ropes attached to a tent is worth examination. If rotted or frayed these ropes ought to be replaced with new. The average strain on a line even in the case of a light-weight tent amounts to fifteen or twenty pounds. You ought to have a safety margin of at least five times this for storms, which may come when least expected.

How a tent is pegged to the ground has quite a lot to do with how it will hold under strain. Many campers make the mistake of driving their pegs either too much on the vertical, or equally bad too much on the horizontal, with the resultant loss of holding power. Pegs should normally be driven at right angles to their subsequent pull. Similarly, sink your guy rope pegs at the right distance out from the wall, not forgetting the element of pull. A corner peg should be driven to divide equally the pull on the tent at its corner angle. And when you tighten up ropes, do so with a view to equalizing strain on the tent as a whole.

When you unroll a packed tent for pitching you sometimes have to fumble around to locate corners, but if you have put a dab of red paint on each corner beforehand they will be easier to find.

In selecting your outfit get the best possible, for the best is none too good, for on the quality of the outfit depends your comfort and in some cases your safety. Better quality will also give you longer wear and better service. The overall cost, in the long run, will probably be less also. Be sure the tent you finally choose embodies all the essentials you will require for your camping trips.

DARK COLOURS ARE BEST

Tents are constructed of many materials ranging from silk and plastic to very heavy canvas. Army canvas is the best, being made of the best materials, and suitable for summer and winter camping. As to colour a white tent will attract insects more than a green or khaki-coloured one and furthermore dark tents are cooler during a hot spell.

In camping as in everyday life sleep is important. The most simple type of camp bed is a ground sheet of rubber or canvas and blankets. The ground sheet should be absolutely waterproof to exclude ground moisture. Woollen blankets are best and should be of a dark colour that will not show dirt easily. A rule to be remembered when sleeping outdoors is that you need as much covering under your body as above.

MOST IMPORTANT

Equipment for the camp depends on the number of persons. One of the most important items is an axe with which to drive in the tent pegs and also for obtaining firewood in case of trouble with the pressure stove. On one occasion while camping in Ireland I had to travel a distance of thirty miles to purchase an axe just because the burner on the stove refused to function. Cooking utensils should be of aluminium and the plates can be of the same metal or of plastic. Ordinary household knives and forks will do and so far as cups and saucers are concerned those made of plastic are ideal. A small first-aid kit should be included in case of accidents and also an electric torch with two or three spare batteries.

Personal kit should contain soap, towels, comb, mirror, toothbrush and paste and also shaving necessities. A waterproof matchbox filled with matches that have also been waterproofed by dipping them in melted paraffin wax is important as is also a good knife with a can opener and strong blade. The knife should be carried on the person at all times.

One of the most important things in a camp is being able to obtain a good supply of fresh water, therefore the site should never be too far away from a supply, and for this task a canvas bucket is needed, but unless you are sure the water is absolutely pure it is best to boil your water for at least ten minutes and scrape off any scum that collects on the top.

Camp cleanliness is very important. A dirty camp is a most unpleasant place and is sure to attract flies and other pests. Burn all rubbish; while empty tins should be flattened with the axe and buried some distance away.

To be able to start a fire in wet weather, always have a supply of dry wood inside the tent as this eliminates the tiresome job of hunting for dry kindling.

On the question of food it is always best to err on the side of plenty rather than go hungry.

Now what about fishing tackle? I always travel light and limit myself to two rods and two reels, for after all too much tackle can become a nuisance. A twelve-foot rod for fishing from rocks and beach and an eight-foot one for boat work and spinning. And talking of boats one of the most pleasant holidays I have ever spent was when a friend brought a boat along. It did not take up much space and we were able to fish good water close inshore. The boat was a second-hand R.A.F. rubber dinghy and accommodated the two of us with ease. With its aid we were able to fish many spots that would have been impossible from rocks, and as a result our sport was greater and much more interesting.

A TASTY CHANGE

Another use to which the dinghy was put was that of prawning during fine weather. Clefts and gullies worn in the rocks by the sea are good places to look for this delightful-to-eat crustacean. Two hours before the tide is at its height is the time to go out after them and the best months are July and August. If you can arrange to do the prawning during the neap tides you will be sure of getting more and bigger prawns. And what a lovely change in the bill of fare to the usual tinned food which the camper has to have.

A long-handled net is needed, the mesh of which is no more than half an inch. Off the Devon and Cornish coast the prawns are particularly large and very sweet when boiled. On occasions I have seen the sea boiling with prawns as they made their way inshore in their search for food, and usually following them are the ravenous bass. So whenever prawns or shrimps are located on a rising tide have the tackle handy because you are sure of some fine sport.

But to get back to tackle. Have a supply of spare hooks and paternosters and also weights and a float or two in case you should come across a shoal of mullet. There is nothing sweeter after a hard day in the open than a nicely fried mullet. Broiled mullet or bass over an open fire is also nice, as a matter of fact most fish are good eating if cooked within a few hours of their capture.

On more than one occasion the writer has taken his camp outfit and spent his holiday in solitary splendour, where long, fatiguing days of fishing and climbing over rocks were followed by a meal before a gay, little camp-fire at that hour when dusk is slipping into darkness and then by restful sleep in the open.

Yes, like many another sportsman whose profession or business is both confining and exacting, I expect much of my brief, annual holiday. A change of scenery and climate are not enough. I want a complete change from my usual mode of living in the town and an opportunity for relaxation that I can find nowhere but camping in some out of the way place where I can hear the surf's heavy and prolonged thunder and the excited squawkings of gulls.

CHAPTER XV

ON THE SEA-SHORE

A great joy to me when my son and daughters were still of school age was to take them wandering along the shore at low tide. Of course at low tide in many places fishing is out of the question so a walk besides filling in the time can be very interesting, especially when you are accompanied by eager-for-knowledge children.

The quiet surface of the sea is broken by wavelets that dance and glance along with the freshening breeze, while a repetition of their forms, in golden light and in shadow, ripples in accompaniment over the corrugated sandy bottom. The eye becomes confused by this interplay of light and shadow, until, more keenly intent it perceives the most impalpable bodies that are making their way through the liquid. Half-globular, opalescent bells of varying sizes are descried among the ripples, either floating aimlessly along, just below the surface, or slightly accelerating their progress by soft contractions. They are jelly fish and faintly violet tints colour the body tissues and help to give substance to this gossamer being that seems fitted to rest upon the surface of some placid lake, rather than to ride the ponderous surges of the sea.

Now another larger body approaches and relies not at all upon the current for its progress, but upon the generous upward reach of its chambered lobed wings and upon their vigorous downward compressions. Measured and even stately are the creature's pulsations while it moves along as if already conscious of the dignity which will attend its pro-maturity for this is the young of the Cyanea chrysaora which in full development is sometimes two and three feet across.

The continual expansion and contractions are thrilling through the bell (body) of the fish and impelling the creature onward, while the tentacles gather in tubular masses underneath the bell, or stream far behind in trailing convolutions, and the quilted draperies that veil the central mouth are also, either extending their tissues to sweep the sand, or sensitively withdrawing them far up beneath the throbbing, pulsing dome.

TAKE CARE

When fishing in jellyfish infested water the angler often gets his tackle covered with the tentacles of the fish. If it is wiped off with the hands be careful not to touch the face with the hands until they have been washed or else you may have a nasty rash. Some jellyfish can be really dangerous to tender skins, the rash which follows the sting of a jellyfish is usually called "sea-nettles".

As we traverse the shore we see an oyster catcher poking away at a pinky-coloured like ball it has found lodged among the rocks. This dapper black and white bird has found a sea urchin and is trying to turn it over so that it can get to the animal inside. On our approach the bird flies off with a shrill cry and we are able to examine the sea urchin more closely. Covering its shell are a number of sharp spikes, but on the underside it is quite bare. In gardens along the Cornish coast you will notice quite a number of sea urchin shells adorning rockeries and real pretty they look. However for the time being this one is safe for we place it in a rock shielded pool from which it will eventually escape when the tide comes in.

A little farther on a little jet of mingled sand and water arrests our attention, and peering closer we see a number of cockles lying half-buried in the damp sand. The cockle can

THE BLACK-BACKED GULL

HERRING GULL

HOODIE CROW

KESTREL

dig a hole for himself, squirt water and also jump. As we proceed to dig out the cockles for bait on a future fishing expedition another squirt of water in the hole we have dug takes place and going deeper we find the razor fish. This fish has an elongated shell sometimes a foot in length.

On the west coast of Scotland they are very plentiful and are excellent bait for all manner of fish.

On the rocks there are numerous conical-shaped shells. These are limpets and as we try to lever one off with a pocket-knife a whelk shell that we thought was empty starts to move. It is a young hermit crab that has taken possession and the vibration of our walking has alarmed him and he is moving to safer quarters.

All about us is sea-weed of various kinds and shells, inhabited and otherwise. Some of the shells are really beautiful in colouring and shape and one of the best is the Livid Top. Of a pinkish colour it has streaks of pearly tints and red dots.

PLEASANT PASTIME

Our progress is stayed by a fresh-water stream that comes splashing down from the rocks and hills beyond. We are in luck because it is in such places that the pearl-bearing mussel likes to breed. By moving a quantity of seaweed large masses of mussels are revealed clinging to the rocks.

Not every mussel holds pearls but if you are lucky you may find a few. They are mostly what is known as seed pearls but on occasions a valuable pearl is discovered. In many inland rivers pearl-bearing mussel beds are known to exist and in these the pearls are a little larger than those from the mussel which inhabits brackish water.

The gulls are now leaving the rocks and moving out to sea which is a sure indication that the tide is on the turn, but before we retrace our steps let us have a look at the birds. That large grey and brown gull is the Herring Gull and like all of his tribe is a proper glutton. The smaller gull with the long black wings is the black-backed and is in my opinion one of the most graceful of all sea birds.

The current estimate of the seagull as an intellectual force is compressed into the word "gullibility"– a verbal monument of contempt. But when we think how many things the gull does that we cannot do – how he has mastered the arts of flying and floating, so that he is equally at home in the air and on the water; how cleverly he adapts himself to his environment, keeping warm among the ice in winter and cool when all the rest of the folks are sweltering in the heat; how well he holds his own against the encroachments of that grasping animal, man, who has driven so many other wild creatures against the wall, and over it into extinction: how prudently he accepts and utilizes all the devices of civilisation which suit him (such as steamship lanes across the Atlantic), without becoming in the least civilised him-self – in short, when we consider how he succeeds in doing what every wise person is trying to do, living his own proper life amid various and changing circumstances, it seems as if we might well reform the spelling of that supercilious word and write it "gullability".

A REAL FRIEND

To me the gull is a friend and what better friend could any angler have than one that locates the fish for him, for wherever fish are feeding near the surface there you will find the gulls in large numbers wheeling, diving and screaming as if they were actually endeavouring to attract the attention of all anglers in the vicinity to come and have a go.

But wait, what is all that commotion on top of the rocks. A number of gulls are mobbing a crow. As the large black-coloured bird dips low over the beach we notice its colouring is not so black as was at first thought. Only its head, throat, wings and tail are black while the rest of its body is a light grey. It is the Hoodie or Grey Crow, a terror to all birds with young. The gulls know his reputation and are taking good care that he shall not settle in their neighbourhood. As the gulls go screaming and chattering after their unwelcome visitor a bird launches itself into the air from high up the rock face. In ever-widening circles it climbs high above the gulls. In colour it is reddish-brown with a few dark spots, the head and tail being grey. It is the Kestrel and no doubt he has his nest in the rocks and is now after a meal.

But we must leave them as the tide is rising fast and we have fishing to do, so, until we meet again – *Tight Lines*.

INDEX

BEGIN FISHING...

Already the author of seven books on fishing (four of which are published in *paperfronts*!), "Uncle" Bill Davies now writes a special book for the younger fisherman about to take out his rod for the first time.

Gone are the days of the bamboo cane and bent pin. Today's angling beginner has at his disposal a bewildering array of tackle, some cheap and some expensive, and as this book shows, a lot more he can make for himself.

In this book he will discover what kind of tackle is needed for each fish, and how to understand the "fishy mind" - one of the secrets of success.

"Uncle Bill" writes from a lifetime of fishing experience; the methods he describes, old and new, are the methods that work.

...WITH UNCLE BILL

PAPERFRONT UNIFORM WITH THIS BOOK

ELLIOT RIGHT WAY BOOKS, KINGSWOOD, SURREY